Asperger
Syndrome
and
Sensory Issues

Asperger Syndrome and Sensory Issues

Practical Solutions for Making Sense of the World

Brenda Smith Myles, Katherine Tapscott Cook,
Nancy E. Miller,
Louann Rinner, and Lisa A. Robbins

Illustrated by
Penny Chiles

Foreword by
Winnie Dunn

AAPC

Autism Asperger Publishing Co.
P.O. Box 23173
Shawnee Mission, Kansas 66283-0173

© 2000 by Autism Asperger Publishing Co.
P.O. Box 23173
Shawnee Mission, Kansas 66283-0173

Publisher's Cataloging-in-Publication
(provided by Quality Books, Inc.)

Myles, Brenda
    Asperger syndrome and sensory issues :
practical solutions for making sense of the world
/ Brenda Myles ... [et al.] – 1st ed.
    p. cm.
    Includes bibliographic references and index.
    Library of Congress Catalog Card Number: 00-132618
    ISBN: 0-9672514-7-8

    1. Asperger's syndrome. 2. Sensorimotor
integration. 3. Asperger's syndrome–Patients–
Psychology. I. Title.

RC553.A88M97 2000   616.89'82
            QBI00-377

This book is designed in Comic Sans and Palatino

Managing Editor: Kirsten McBride
Cover Design: Taku Hagiwara
Production Assistant: Ginny Biddulph
Interior Design/Production: Tappan Design

Printed in the United States of America

*This book is dedicated
to the children, parents,
and educators who have
been our teachers.*

Just Get to Know Me

Flourescent lights, too bright, blinding like the western sun
Playground chaotic, like city streets, people run, run, run
Instructions, too many, clog the system, like a paper jam
IEPs, Ascertainment, Level 5, who the hell gives a damn
I'm drowning here, can't anyone see
But you're too busy worrying about 'me'

A pencil drops, a classmate coughs, distractions a
full scale emergency
Teacher's away? You say! Who are you? Who am I?
Escalating anxiety
Change desk. Changed your mind. It changed my life, what a mess
No math today, you say. Instead we might play? Stress! STRESS!
I'm sinking here, help me please
But you're too busy worrying about the IEPs

Can't concentrate, want time out, have to get away
I ask for space, you decide I have to stay
Thump the desk, clench my fists, feels like slow motion
Push the desk over, kick the door, out, out from the commotion
I can't breathe, unlock my lungs, please give me the key
But you're too busy worrying about my 'identity'

Somebody please, please, please
I'm dying here, from a new disease
Overdone Ascertainment, Level 5 IEP
And not enough one on one, just get to know me

Josie Santomauro, 2000
Brisbane, Australia

Note. In the Australian school system, Ascertainment is a primary stage of the IEP. The system includes level of need, with 6 being indicative of the greatest need. Once a child has obtained Ascertainment and a level, an IEP can be written.

Josie is a mother of two; her son was diagnosed with Asperger Syndrome in 1994 at the age of five. She has worked within the primary school environment as a teacher aide, secretary and library aide. Josie is currently a full-time writer and is completing her graduate certification in creative writing at Queensland University of Technology, Brisbane, Australia.

FOREWORD

Imagine all the ways that we might describe the experiences of living across a span of 50 years. In some ways, perspectives become more complex as we become increasingly aware of more and more aspects of living. But in other ways, across this length of time, the simplicity and rhythm of living become more apparent. In addition, both of these ways of characterizing living would be different from the way in which we would have characterized each of the decades within the 50 years, because the accumulation of knowledge and insight informs us in a unique way from any other single experience. When we can move forward and backward in our thinking about phenomena, patterns can emerge that were not evident in our actual experience of them as individual parts.

We are experiencing this same 50-year perspective when examining and addressing the issues of Asperger Syndrome. In 1944 Hans Asperger provided an initial description of a group of children who were unique from any others he had encountered. In the 50 years since then, professionals have increasingly recognized the uniqueness and complexity of this disorder. As a result, Asperger Syndrome has been included in the *Diagnostic and Statistical Manual of Mental Disorders-4th Revision* (American Psychiatric Association, 1994). Although the core behaviors that contribute to the diagnosis of Asperger Syndrome have remained surprisingly constant, professionals have continued to search for underlying factors that might be present to yield these core behaviors. Professionals have believed that by understanding underlying factors we have more precise options for effective intervention to support successful and satisfying lives for persons with Asperger Syndrome and their families.

For example, in the last decade particularly, professionals have begun to interpret some core behaviors of Asperger Syndrome as indicative of difficulties with sensory processing. I don't think it is any coincidence that these hypotheses emerged during the "Decade of the Brain," a period in our culture during which we have focused on neuroscience to explain many human phenomena. From a sensory processing point of view, core behaviors such as "difficulty discerning relevant from irrelevant stimuli" might indicate the person's inability to screen incoming sensory information properly for use in daily life.

In order to advance knowledge, we will have to test these hypotheses. We have to create systematic methods for applying a sensory processing perspective to the daily life challenges of persons with Asperger Syndrome and measure the effectiveness of these methods. Families and persons with Asperger Syndrome must understand the hypotheses in their own terms so that they can be informed participants, and provide insights about their own lived experiences. Family and persons with Asperger Syndrome provide the 50-year perspective, because they can reflect forward and backward as they consider the ideas of sensory processing, and give us insights we cannot gain from merely observing.

This book contributes to knowledge development by providing friendly explanations about complex phenomena. This approach invites families to participate in the perspective taking, so they can share both the complexity and the rhythms of living that come along with the experience of Asperger Syndrome with those of us who are merely observers (i.e., the professionals). Only with all the perspectives can we hope to expose the truth.

Winnie Dunn, Ph.D., OTR, FAOTA

Winnie Dunn, Ph.D., OTR, FAOTA, is professor and chair of the Department of Occupational Therapy Education at the University of Kansas. She has written many books and articles on service provision in schools and on sensory processing in daily life. In 1999, her research on sensory processing with children culminated in the publication of the Sensory Profile, *a caregiver reporting measure of children's responses to sensory events in daily life. She continues this work with infants, toddlers, adults and older adults, currently collecting standardization and validation data nationwide. Most recently, she has authored or coauthored two books about best practices:* Best Practice Occupational Therapy in Community Settings with Children and Families, *and* Measuring Occupational Performance: A Guide to Best Practice Assessment, *both published by SLACK.*

Dr. Dunn has received many honors throughout her career. She was named Fellow of the American Occupational Therapy Association (FAOTA) and received the Award of Merit for significant contributions to the profession. She was named to the Academy of Research of the American Occupational Therapy Foundation, and has received research awards from her university as well. In the spring of 2000, she was named the Eleanor Clark Slagle Lecturer for 2001, the highest honor given in the profession, for her significant contributions to knowledge development.

TABLE OF CONTENTS

INTRODUCTION

Parents typically "know" the unique characteristics of their children and are often able to anticipate their own child's actions based on what they know about children in general. Some children, however, offer challenges that make it difficult for teachers and parents to anticipate how they may react to certain situations. That is, the reactions of some children tend to vary based on a number of different factors – time of day, level of stress and types of demands made on the child. You may recognize some of the characteristics illustrated in Figure I.1 as typical of some of the children you know. Some children experience several of these problems while others may experience one or two. Whether the child demonstrates one or a multitude of puzzling behaviors, trying to find an explanation helps you not only to make sense of what is occurring but also to anticipate similar reactions in the future.

While some behaviors and reactions are problematic and interfere with work or play, others result in successful interactions. What is the difference and how can we help reduce or eliminate the occurrence of ineffective behaviors? This book will cover puzzling behaviors exhibited by children and youth with Asperger Syndrome that may have a sensory base.

Chapter 1 begins with an overview of sensory integration terminology and a discussion of how the sensory systems impact behavior. Chapter 2 takes an indepth look at the sensory issues reported to be associated with Asperger Syndrome. In Chapter 3 we review several formal and informal assessment tools that can assist you in pinpointing sensory characteristics. Chapter 4 offers a series of interventions in the sensory areas, including specific behaviors, possible reasons for their occurrence, and strategies that may help promote home, school, and community success for children and youth with Asperger Syndrome. Finally, Chapter 5 presents a case study outlining the sensory assessment of and subsequent programming for a child with Asperger Syndrome.

This book attempts to explain how many children with Asperger Syndrome (AS) relate to the world through their senses. To understand the sensory systems can be a complex task. Through the use of

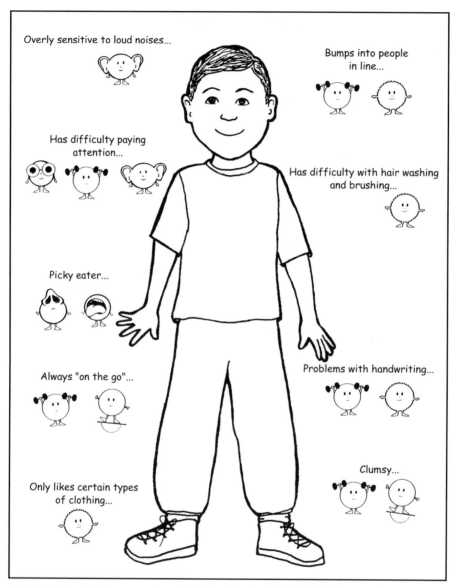

Figure I.1. Sample of sensory characteristics of the typical child with Asperger Syndrome.

the SENSORY GANG, we have tried to reduce the complexity of this topic. The SENSORY GANG appear throughout the book providing information in a user-friendly fashion. We hope you enjoy the SENSORY GANG and that they help you understand the needs of the child or youth with AS.

THE SENSORY GANG

Ms. Tactile

People say I am so touchy-feely! I can't help it! From head to toe and all over, my skin keeps me "in touch" with the world. Even inside my mouth I feel things – light touch, deep pressure, hard or soft, sharp or dull, vibration, temperature and ohhhhh … the pain!

Mr. Vestibular

I keep everything "right with the world"! Because of me, you can deal with gravity when you are moving, no matter the direction or speed. Even when standing or sitting still, I am very important because of my sense of balance. Posture and muscle tone depend on the signals I interpret from the inner ear.

Ms. Proprioception

I do more that just push and pull, flex and stretch, pry and press! Information coming from my joints, muscles and tendons helps me adjust my body position for smooth movements with just the "right amount" of pressure. People say I am important for good "motor planning" when this information is accurate.

We three, Ms. T, Mr. V, and Ms. P,
are a pretty tight group. Some say we
are the foundation of the sensory system gang.
Who and what we stand for is even greater
when the rest of the gang is integrated!

Ms. Visual

I've got my eyes on you! I am on the lookout to deliver valuable details about what I see. Color, contrast, line, shape, form and movement have a part in how you perceive the world. My messages (with the collaboration of my friends) help determine what to pay attention to and what to ignore as well as help direct your actions and movements.

Ms. Auditory

Do you hear what I hear? I don't mean to whine but I can get your attention too. Listen to me, please, I'm all ears. It's not just about volume – consider also tone, pitch, rhythm and sequence of sounds. Processing me can be difficult but it is necessary if I am to be understood. If I don't have the others, help out, I'm just noise … sigh.

Mr. Gustatory

Ah, to savor the "sweet taste of success," or was it bitter or salty? Maybe sour or spicy? Taste buds and saliva are the grounds for my great sensory contributions. I often get no respect but one thing's for sure, I know "what I like!" By the way, I am intricately linked with Ms. Olfactory.

Ms. Olfactory

Although some consider me not as refined as my other sensory friends, I go way back in time – kind of a survival thing. Strong memories are associated with certain smells. I subjectively consider the odor, especially when Mr. Gustatory is around. Remember, the "nose knows" and … "Don't forget to stop and smell the roses."

Chapter
1

SENSORY PROCESSING

Sensation, that is, what we can see, hear, feel, smell, and taste, gives us information about the environment around us and about ourselves. It helps us understand the world and how to act on and within it. If we compare our bodies to a computer, our central nervous system or brain is the central processing unit (CPU) that receives, interprets, organizes, and sends messages to the rest of the body. Our central nervous system or brain helps us to regard, disregard, seek out, or avoid sensation to maintain or increase feelings of comfort, excitement, rest, and positive interactions with objects and people. It also influences how we try to avoid that which is painful, uncomfortable, or stressful. Whether it's cold outside, we have a stomachache, our shoes are too tight, or the food smells putrid, the way we interpret and perceive those sensations helps us determine what actions we take. Further, the results of those actions and associated feelings contribute to our sense of well-being, whether positive or negative.

Our interpretation of sensation is individual. As a result, reactions to a given sensation (behavior) can be very different among people even when they experience the same sensory information. For example, you may love Mexican food, but your spouse finds it too spicy and upsetting to his stomach. Your brother likes loud rock-and-roll tunes and you prefer soft classical music. Although each person's brain directs and is in charge of this interpretation, much of the process occurs at an automatic level without cognitive awareness of what is taking place.

The complexity of the central nervous system seems quite abstract. Yet, neuroscientists can show evidence that sensory input evokes physiological changes in the body. Sometimes we observe these changes in persons who seem to react strongly to everyday sensory input. For example, a child who smells a teacher's perfume may feel nauseous. He may begin to sweat and his facial color may change.

1

Other changes may be less obvious although still detectable as in the increased heart rate of a child who clings to you after hearing the neighbor's dog barking loudly.

Even before a child is born, her brain, or central nervous system, is working to organize sensory information. This flow of sensory information may be subtle or intense, frequent or sporadic, or fleeting or long-lasting. For example, to the unborn baby, movement and position changes within the mother's body, the temperature of the amniotic fluid, the feel of a thumb within the mouth, and the sounds of the outside world are all information bits that may contribute to the developing central nervous system. This is why some mothers play classical music or read aloud while pregnant to stimulate growth and development of the fetus' sensory nervous system.

Dr. A. Jean Ayres (1979), an occupational therapist, defined sensory integration as "the organization of sensation for use" (p. 5). The typically developing central nervous system involves ongoing, dynamic interplay and comparison of information from all sensory systems. The outcomes of this process are seen in the responses we make to given situations and reflect multiple contributing factors.

Consider the perspective of one student in a classroom where cooperative learning groups are used to teach social studies content. As all four groups plan and develop their projects, our student can hear the children's voices from all groups to some degree. Focusing on the verbal direction of his group leader and moving to the floor where a variety of materials can be spread out, he realizes that he needs his colored pencils to work on a map. Balancing on his knees and right hand, he reaches into his desk to retrieve his pencil box with his left hand. At that moment a friend directs a question to him, pointing to a graph in the social studies book. As our student looks at the book, he shifts his weight and continues the search for the pencil with his left hand. Feeling the clasp of the pencil box and pushing just hard enough to pop it open, he moves his fingers over crayons, an eraser, paper brads, and other miscellaneous objects until he feels the pencils bundled together by a rubber band. The series of adaptive responses demonstrated by the student in this situation reflect the effective integration of different types of sensation.

In contrast, given the same classroom and learning activity, another student may find it impossible to filter out the noise from other

2

groups, making it difficult to focus on the task or be an effective contributor to the cooperative group assignment. The sensory input in the environment may be overwhelming to this specific child to the point that he withdraws and covers his ears. This response is an attempt by the student to alleviate some discomfort, but it limits his learning possibilities through interactions with peers and manipulation of materials. As a result, the effective integration of sensation necessary for an adaptive response has not occurred.

The previous examples illustrate the link between the sensory input and behaviors that result accordingly. Exactly how that link occurs and the words chosen to describe the process may be expressed in different ways by different individuals or groups of people who attempt to identify and explain behavior using a sensory processing perspective (Miller & Lane, 2000). In other words, a neuroscientist uses words that are intended to refer to a specific neurophysiological action whereas an occupational therapist may use the same or similar term in a more global manner. As the theory of sensory processing continues to evolve and the scientific community learns more about how the central nervous system works, additional terminology will emerge.

While it is beyond the scope of this book to give a comprehensive presentation of sensory integration theory, we will examine some of the hypothesized components of the process in a simplified manner to help bring about understanding and insight into the behaviors you observe. The information that follows is an attempt to explain some of the components of sensory processing and how we can use that understanding to make "sense" of our own behaviors and those of others, including children with Asperger Syndrome.

The Sensory Systems

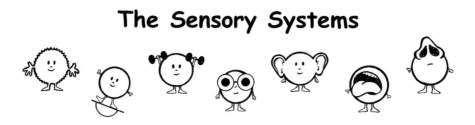

The individual sensory systems' (tactile, vestibular, proprioceptive, visual, auditory, gustatory, olfactory) receptors, or specialized cells, throughout the body provide the starting points for delivering messages to the central nervous system (see Table 1.1). Some parts of the body have an increased density or number of these receptors compared to other parts of the body. Your mouth and hands, for example, have more receptors in the same amount of body surface than your back or leg, providing more sensory messages for processing. Passive and active experiences and interactions with the environment provide sensory input that is delivered throughout the central nervous system. As messages travel along neural pathways, specific regions of the brain compare or combine information from other areas. Figure 1.1 illustrates the sensory reaction that may occur as a child touches a slimy substance such as Gak™, Floam™, or Bugs n' Goo™. Other children happily anticipate playing with the slimy substance, while the boy in the middle of this example appears anxious and even nauseous at the mere thought of having to touch the material.

Figure 1.1. Sensory reactions to a slimy substance.

Table 1.1

Location and Functions of the Sensory Systems

System	Location	Function
Tactile (touch)	**Skin** – density of cell distribution varies through-out the body. Areas of greatest density include mouth, hands, and genitals.	Provides information about the environment and object qualities (touch, pressure, texture, hard, soft, sharp, dull, heat, cold, pain).
Vestibular (balance)	**Inner ear** – stimulated by head movements and input from other senses, especially visual.	Provides information about where our body is in space, and whether or not we or our sur-roundings are moving. Tells about speed and direction of movement.
Proprioception (body awareness)	**Muscles and joints** – activated by muscle contractions and movement.	Provides information about where a certain body part is and how it is moving.
Visual (sight)	**Retina of the eye** – stimulated by light.	Provides information about objects and persons. Helps us define boundaries as we move through time and space.
Auditory (hearing)	**Inner ear** – stimulated by air/sound waves.	Provides information about sounds in the environment (loud, soft, high, low, near, far).
Gustatory (taste)	**Chemical receptors in the tongue** – closely entwined with the olfactory (smell) system.	Provides information about different types of taste (sweet, sour, bitter, salty, spicy).
Olfactory (smell)	**Chemical receptors in the nasal structure** – closely associated with the gustatory system.	Provides information about differ-ent types of smell (musty, acrid, putrid, flowery, pungent).

When we have a sensory experience, the brain interprets the experience in one of two ways: discriminative or protective. These two functions form the basis for future sensory experiences.

Discrimination

Each of the systems has a *mapping* component that supplies details for the central nervous system to consider. This is also known as *discrimination*. For example, when a person touches (tactile) an object, the mapping function of the tactile system provides information about where the touch is occurring (the hand, not the back of the thigh) as well as whether the object is hard, soft, fuzzy, smooth, round, angular, and so on. Accurate information about these details helps us interpret the object in an effective and useful manner, whether it means to hold it without squishing it (if it is a ripe peach) or to grasp it firmly (as in preparing to serve a tennis ball).

Protective Function

The sensory systems also have a protective function that helps to keep us away from danger or harm. For example, when we reach into a boot and detect something soft and fuzzy, the tactile system may signal us to move our hand quickly to keep from being bitten by a brown recluse spider. The central nervous system operates in a way that seeks to maintain a state of equilibrium. If sensory information starts to interfere with this state, the neurological system may generate a protective "fright, flight, or fight" response or reaction. This reaction is often accompanied by physiological responses to support survival from other parts of the body such as sweating, dilation of pupils, or an increased heart rate. Sensory inputs have the potential to evoke a number of reactions. And those reactions are seen as behaviors. In other words, the behaviors that we see (and don't see) in somebody come from what and how that person sees, feels, hears, or otherwise senses.

The Sensory Integration Process

As mentioned earlier, in order to "make sense" of all the sensations we experience, they must be integrated. The individual sensory systems operate in a similar manner. First, we *register* or become aware of the sensation. Then we *orient* or pay attention to it. Next, we attempt to *interpret* the sensation by using current information and referencing past experiences for comparison. *Organization* occurs when our brain decides what we should do in response to the sensation. The final step is *execution* or what we actually do in response to a sensation.

Although this process is simplistically presented here, this is not a simple start-stop process, nor is the distinction between the steps clear-cut. The steps are lodged in our brains and we use the information when we repeat familiar experiences as well as when we come into contact with new situations. The sensory systems send information to act upon and interact with other parts of the brain. For example, the limbic or emotional system may be involved. When touching a hot pan, feelings associated with that experience are also stored. Finally, cognition may impact the response. The individual who touched the pan may think, "I should have used a potholder. I know better than to pick up a hot pan with my bare hands."

Let us now look at each of the five steps of the sensory integration process in more detail.

Registration

As mentioned, *registration* refers to an awareness. This awareness level or threshold is the point in the integration process where we "know" that we have touched, tasted, smelled, and so on. This threshold has to be reached before the central nervous system can consider further action. To complicate matters, we all have different awareness levels or thresholds. "With a low threshold, the nervous system responds frequently to stimuli because it does not take very much input to reach the threshold and activate the system. With high thresholds, the nervous system does not respond to stimuli because it takes a lot of input to reach a threshold ..." (Dunn, 1999, p. 32). Subsequently, the "strength" or amount of the sensory input necessary to trigger further action is also variable among individuals.

To further complicate things, these awareness levels fluctuate depending on time of day, degree of stress, our emotional state, physical health, and level of hunger. Other influencing factors may include genetic predisposition, environmental influences, and past interactive experiences with the world. It is also possible to have a low threshold for a particular sense and a high threshold for another. For example, Ali has a low threshold for flowery scents; he notices immediately when his teacher wears White Gardenia cologne. At the same time, he has a high threshold for spicy foods; he can eat habañera peppers without reacting a bit.

Threshold patterns continue throughout life. When she arrives home, Beth announces that as she was driving from the library, she heard a funny noise in the car. Her husband, Charlie, who is watching a football game, is so intent on processing the football game that he does not even register, or hear, Beth talking. While Charlie is watching the football game, his threshold for other specific auditory input (hearing his wife) is high. That is, Beth has to raise her voice or increase the intensity of her message to be heard.

People can also demonstrate low thresholds for registering information. For example, when the Oprah Winfrey show is on, Phoebe sends her kids out to play. She considers this hour her only time to relax. If her children are playing in front of the television, she is distracted and cannot concentrate on the show. Her sensory threshold for auditory input is low, which may trigger an emotional response. That is, Phoebe is likely to become agitated and raise her voice to the children if they disturb her.

Thresholds occur along a continuum. Charlie, at one end of the continuum, appears to be hyposensitive or underresponsive to the registration of Beth's voice. At the other end of the continuum, Phoebe, during Oprah, is hypersensitive or overresponsive to the registration of her children's voices.

Charlie and Phoebe's reactions change throughout the day depending on a variety of things. During the televised news, Charlie can help his son with his homework and Phoebe can talk on the phone. Both get the gist of the news, falling somewhere in the middle of the continuum. Figure 1.2 shows a threshold continuum.

Orientation

Orientation typically occurs after registration. At this stage there is a focus on the input, that is, we regard or attend to someone talking, something touching us, or something we smell. A shift in attention from another input may result. For example, while watching television, Charlie does not notice Beth's voice, as he is totally engrossed in the football game. Similarly, during Oprah, Phoebe is oriented toward the television host and her guests. She does not hear or orient toward the "normal" sounds of her children playing in the backyard. At this stage, our brains decide what to pay attention to and what to ignore.

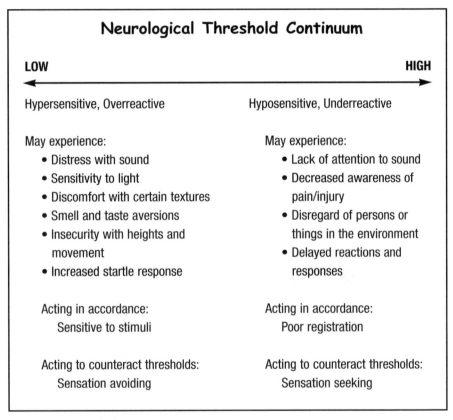

Figure 1.2. Neurological threshold continuum.

Interpretation

Interpretation takes place when we relate our past experiences to what is happening now. These experiences may include emotions, memories, and even things we have said. During the football game, Charlie does not register or orient toward anything Beth says, until she utters the word "transmission." At that instant registration, orientation, and interpretation all occur at the same time. Charlie remembers – not too fondly – how he felt when the last Mastercard bill arrived and the ensuing argument with Beth over the condition of her car.

As Oprah introduces her second guest, Phoebe registers and orients toward her children in the backyard. Her youngest child, Michael, always accident-prone, has begun to cry. Upon hearing him, Phoebe's interpretation is that something serious must have happened – the last time he cried like that he required three stitches. Phoebe is suddenly alarmed.

An important part of interpretation is the "fright, flight, fight" reaction that occurs to protect us. When Charlie registers and orients toward the word "transmission," his interpretation is one of "fright, flight, fight." He feels the strong need to protect their financial security. His heart rate and breathing increase, his face turns red, and he prepares an emotional response (see Figure 1.3).

Phoebe, upon hearing Michael's cry, experiences a similar reaction but for different reasons. Her heart rate and respiration increase and she prepares for a physical response (see Figure 1.4).

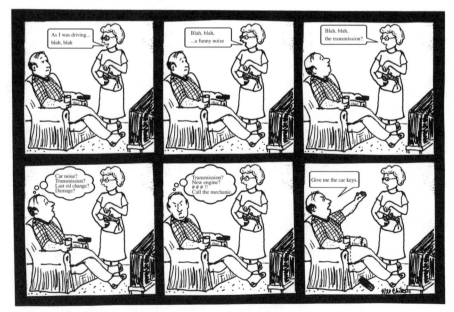

Figure 1.3. Charlie moves through the sensory integration process.

Figure 1.4. Phoebe moves through the sensory integration process.

Organization

Organization occurs when we determine if a response to a given event is necessary and what, if any response, we will make. In response to Beth's reference to the car transmission, Charlie figures that he needs to take an investigative role in determining the extent of any damage that may already have occurred. His facial muscles tense and he prepares to take action.

As Michael cries, Phoebe organizes a response that involves jumping up off of the couch, pushing the screen door open and taking the steps two at a time off the deck. This will enable her to get to Michael as soon as possible to determine the reason for his crying and Michael's needs.

Execution of a Response

The final stage in the sensory integration process involves an emotion or carrying out an action or *response*. This could include a response to do nothing! Ignoring is considered the execution of a response.

Charlie responds to Beth's utterance of the word "transmssion" with the following, "We're already broke. This car is going to send us to the poor house." As he holds out his hand, he loudly and slowly says, "Give me the $%#@ car keys and I'll take a look." He has executed a response that will most likely result in a reaction from Beth.

Phoebe's execution of a response includes running to the backyard and yelling, "It's okay, honey, mommy is coming." Phoebe scans the environment to find the source of the problem. She also scans Michael to attempt to determine what is wrong.

Summary

The sensory integration process is never-ending and the events are not separate. One event influences another and so on. For example, in Charlie's case, the third time Beth reports problems with her car, Charlie's response is likely to register higher on the Richter scale than the first or second time. In the same way, Phoebe's responses to Michael are also not discrete. After a series of accidents, Phoebe's responses escalate. Charlie's and Phoebe's movement through the steps of the sensory integration process was illustrated in Figures 1.3 and 1.4, respectively.

In real life, the process from registration to execution of a response often occurs in less than a second. We are typically not aware of the individual stages since they happen in a quick and flowing manner.

Modulation

Some sensory messages or input have a facilitating effect on our overall nervous system, resulting in a state of alertness or readiness to respond. Other sensory messages may be disregarded or inhibited, decreasing the possibilities that a response will occur. Modulation is the critical balance or regulation of facilitating and inhibiting effects. When a person is aware that she needs either to energize or calm down, she may choose a sensory strategy to facilitate or inhibit sensory messages. For example, when you start to feel tired on a long drive, you might chew gum, drink something cold, or turn up the radio to become more alert. Other messages reduce or inhibit the nervous system, resulting in a decreased response. For example, to calm your child before going to bed, you might read her a story, give her a warm bath, or play a quiet game.

When modulation is intact, the nervous system responds to some input from the senses while disregarding other input. Therefore, with effective modulation, we can balance our reaction so that it matches the requirement of the situation. This balance enables us to recognize the familiarity of some input without attending to it in a way that would detract from our intended focus or task. We say that *habituation* occurs when the familiar input does not require additional attention. An example might be the person who can sustain his focus on study-ing for a test while the neighbor is mowing the lawn. In this case, habituation to the sound of the lawn mower is necessary for optimal focus on the test material.

Other input may require enhanced attention because it is potential-ly important. When sensory messages are familiar but require addi-tional attention, sensitization to that input may occur. A young child engaged in a preschool center activity is aware that the lights in the room have gone out. Although she can still see the play food, sensiti-zation to lights out at this time will help her determine if it is an emer-gency situation or if this is the transition cue for the next activity. Her enhanced attention to this sensory input will help her determine the appropriate response or action. Again, successful modulation in the brain maintains a sense of harmony and balance. An analogy to mod-ulation is the symphony conductor who directs each instrumental sec-tion to achieve an overall effect.

Effective Sensory Processing

Most of the time the sensory integration process is effective. That is, we take in information, process it, and act on it appropriately. We reg-ister, orient, interpret, and execute a response in a manner that is well matched to the situation. Our brain's regulation or modulation of sen-sory messages supports that effective performance by further inte-grating the information to result in a behavior or action that matches our intent. The quality of the behavior or action is feedback to the cen-tral nervous system that illustrates whether or not effective processing has occurred. The sought-after balance does not mean that we don't demonstrate loud or excitable responses. Conversely, we may exhibit low-key reactions in words or movement.

At a basketball game, for example, Maria, an individual with typical sensory processing, jumps up and down, shakes her fist, and screams as a basket is made by "her team." These reactions reflect how she feels about the event. If Maria exhibits these behaviors following a basket made by the opposing team, her response may be due to a perceived injustice resulting from an undetected or overlooked foul. Or her actions may be motivated by the intent to distract, threaten, or otherwise set the opposing team players and their fans off guard.

Similar behaviors might be seen in the case of an emergency when a "fright, flight, fight" response is necessary to preserve a person's well-being. For example, jumping up and down, shaking one's fist and screaming may stop the unwanted advances of an inebriated reveler at a St. Patrick's Day Parade.

Effective sensory processing contributes to motor planning abilities or "praxis," which is necessary for Maria to execute body actions regardless of her motivations. Motor planning includes:

- coming up with an idea about the action
- having an accurate sense of where the body is
- starting the action
- executing the steps in the appropriate sequence
- making adjustments as needed
- knowing when to stop the action

Although all of the sensory systems play a contributing part in motor planning, input from the tactile, vestibular, and proprioceptive systems is considered to have the greatest influence on performance. Thus, accurate processing of sensory information impacts an individual's ability to effectively plan motor activities in a coordinated manner.

Maria's bleacher seat behind the backboard affords her a great position for attempting to distract the opposing team player when he steps to the free-throw line to take a shot. When the foul shot is called, she stands with her feet up to the edge of the bleacher step and brings her hands up to her face to cup them around her mouth as she prepares to scream. The fans around her rise too, bumping into her. She draws one of her feet back and shifts her weight to provide a more stable base of support. The fan on her right leans into Maria with her arms extended in the air. Maria quickly picks up on the back-and-forth sway of the surrounding crowd as she adjusts her feet once again and extends her arms to join in the rhythmical "wave." Because Maria has effective sensory processing skills that contribute to good motor planning, she efficiently demonstrates this action in a coordinated way.

In other situations, an individual who has typical sensory processing may demonstrate more restrained responses. When talking to a friend while working in the library, Malcolm speaks in a hushed voice, perhaps partially covering his mouth with his hands. He also moves slowly while getting up so as not to disturb others with the scraping of the chair legs. Preparing to leave, Malcolm zips his backpack slowly, again to keep the noise down. He is aware of the overstuffed backpack and walks around the perimeter of the library stacks instead of taking the shortcut through the narrow aisles where it would be likely to bump others or knock books off shelves. Those same behaviors might prove helpful if Malcolm needs to escape danger or, at the very least, avoid an unwelcome encounter. Responding in a way so as to remain undetected is often desirable as when rounding the corner and inadvertently walking toward what appears to be a heated discussion between Paul and his girlfriend who are standing in front of their lockers. In either situation, Malcolm's effective motor planning abilities enable him to come up with a strategy that is appropriate for the situation.

Individuals with effective sensory processing often demonstrate strong sensory preferences.

While individuals with effective sensory processing can demonstrate a range of responses appropriate to the given situation, they may demonstrate strong sensory preferences. Preferences are often reflected in choice of work, hobby or leisure options. Using the individuals in the previous example, Maria likes her job as a package handler. It is active work in a noisy environment but the part-time position allows her to attend the local community college and play softball on a recreational team. This lifestyle is compatible with one who seeks sensory input. On the other hand, Malcolm's after-school routine includes watching TV for 60 to 90 minutes while reclining on the couch. During this time he likes to pile the cushions and pillows on top of himself to feel the weight. Malcolm has recently started watching golf tournaments on TV, too, as he is starting to learn the game from his father. Malcolm's choices reflect his need to limit or control amounts and types of sensory input to be comfortable. Both Maria and Malcolm demonstrate sensory processing abilities that enable them to be successful at a variety of tasks; however, their choices reflect activities with inherent characteristics that best match their sensory preferences.

Children who process sensory information effectively are often responsive to home routines, manage successfully in community settings, and are frequently viewed favorably by teachers at school. Such children:

- can continue their play in the yard without being bothered by the noise of the lawn mower, weeder, or edge trimmer
- eat a variety of foods although preferences may be evident
- accompany their parents as they make their way through the crowd to find a place at the curb to wait for the parade to begin, without reacting to the close proximity of other people
- tolerate the singing and dancing of the staff at the restaurant where grandma and grandpa like to take them
- finish their seatwork because they do not orient toward the noises of children on the playground
- complete their assignments because they follow verbal directions and can sit for an extended period of time

Ineffective Sensory Processing

Individuals with ineffective sensory processing can experience problems in one or more of the sensory areas or at any point in the sensory integration process. If there are difficulties with effective registration of sensory input, then subsequent steps in the integration process will be disrupted. Jerome, a child with an ear infection, may have a restricted range of hearing. His limited ability to register sound in all ranges affects what sounds he orients toward. Another child, Isabelle, registers sensation but has difficulty orienting to the appropriate sensory stimulus. If orientation toward a particular sensory stimulus does not occur, it cannot be interpreted and therefore the rest of the sensory integration process is negatively impacted.

Poor modulation of input may result in responses that are not balanced to meet the situation. Individuals who have modulation difficulties often under- or overreact to situations. Underreaction is evident in Nan's response to certain tactile stimuli. For example, she wears her socks so that they are bunched up inside her shoes with no apparent discomfort. On the other hand, Nan is overreactive to the auditory sense. She cannot tolerate it when her husband smacks his lips when he eats. Some individuals perceive harmless sensory input as threatening and potentially dangerous. Sam responds to the sound of the vacuum cleaner by covering his ears, crying, and running to his room. This is clearly a more extreme response than typically demonstrated by effective sensory precessors. Misinterpretation of Sam's behavior may lead the observer to regard his response as strong-willed or immature rather than recognizing it as a "fright, flight, fight" response.

Motor planning problems can impact an individual's ability to participate in sports, carry a lunch tray, open a milk carton, tie shoes, or ride a bicycle. It took Taylor a long time to learn to get on his bike by swinging his leg up over the wheel and the seat. Even now, it requires considerable concentration for him to complete this step. Thus, his parents have observed him talking himself through getting on his bike. Taylor's knees are often scraped because he inadvertently hits them against the tire as he mounts his bike. Even with training wheels, Taylor is not an accomplished bicyclist. His feet fall from the pedals as he pedals, he has difficulty moving his feet in the correct direction to brake, and he often steps too hard or too soft on the brake. However, he has learned a strategy for braking – he puts his feet down to stop after guiding his bike to the grass as he knows the grass provides a soft landing and an easier way to stop. Taylor's bicycle riding skills frustrate his father, who is anxious to remove Taylor's training wheels so that they can bike together. His father is also concerned because his son is the only eight-year-old on the block who cannot ride a bicycle.

Children who have sensory processing difficulties often experience challenges in home, community, and school settings. This might be seen in children who:

- cannot tolerate clothing that feels "stiff or scratchy," such as jeans or certain synthetic-blend fabrics
- resist brushing their teeth because they gag when the toothbrush touches their lips
- refuse to climb playground equipment or attempt to swing during an outing to the park
- limit what sections of the grocery store to enter, avoiding the seafood and meat aisles because of frequent strong odors
- react strongly when someone brushes against them in line or constantly move around in their seat
- look at the teacher when she talks, but have difficulty screening out irrelevant stimuli such as the buzz of the overhead fluorescent lights

Summary

Our sensory systems work together to help us understand our world. When the tactile, vestibular, proprioceptive, visual, auditory, gustatory, and olfactory systems work as they are supposed to, we (a) act and react to situations effectively, (b) learn, (c) make friends, and (d) stay away from harmful things. Ineffective sensory systems can have an equally profound and negative effect. That is, when our systems don't work as they are supposed to, our entire lives are impacted. As a result, we can experience problems (a) paying attention, (b) learning, and (c) understanding the intentions of others. In addition, we may overreact or underreact to situations.

When we understand how our sensory systems work, we can better understand why we do the things we do or act the way we do. In short, our sensory systems help us "make sense" of the world.

Chapter 2

ASPERGER SYNDROME AND ASSOCIATED SENSORY CHARACTERISTICS

In what follows, I will describe a particularly interesting and highly recognisable type of child. The children I will present all have in common a fundamental disturbance which manifests itself in their physical appearance, expressive functions and, indeed, their whole behavior. (Asperger, 1944, p. 37)

With these words Hans Asperger (1944) began to describe the characteristics of children he termed as having "autistic psychopathy." We have come to recognize these children as having Asperger Syndrome. Although Asperger did his work in the mid-1940s, we are still trying to understand this exceptionality. To date, we know that individuals with Asperger Syndrome (AS) typically demonstrate:

- average to above-average intelligence
- social and communication deficits
- obsessive and narrowly defined interests
- concrete and literal thinking
- inflexibility
- problem-solving and organizational problems
- difficulty in discerning relevant from irrelevant stimuli
- behavioral issues that are often related to lack of understanding,

stress, or a defensive panic reaction (Asperger, 1944; Attwood, 1998; Myles & Simpson, 1998; Myles, Simpson, & Bock, 2000; Myles & Southwick, 1999; Wing, 1981).

While there are exceptions to these characteristics within individuals with AS, we accept these traits as common to the exceptionality. *The Diagnostic and Statistical Manual of Mental Disorders – 4th Revision* (American Psychiatric Association, 1994) and the *International Classification of Diseases and Related Health Problems – 10th Edition* (World Health Organization, 1992) attempt to quantify and standardize the diagnostic criteria for AS (see Tables 2.1 and 2.2). These documents represent the best information we have; however, the framers of these documents, as well as those who work and live with individuals who have AS, recognize that there is much more to learn. The depth of our knowledge is still so superficial that it will be years before we gain a full understanding of the characteristics that have come to be associated with the work of Hans Asperger.

One area that we have just begun to explore relates to our senses. Although Hans Asperger described the sensory difficulties of the children he observed, current researchers and practitioners have largely ignored this aspect of his work. In fact, until recently no research articles had been published on the sensory issues in AS, suggesting that the sensory area does not impact the functioning of children with this syndrome.

But we may have been wrong. Given recent evidence, parents who live with, and practitioners who work with, individuals with AS are justified in exclaiming a resounding "I told you so," for all of the times they have anecdotally reported the sensory problems their children or students experienced.

A study of 42 children and youth with AS by Myles, Dunn, and Orr (2000) supports sensory processing as a distinct problem area. In fact, more than 50% of children and youth with AS had difficulties in the auditory, vestibular, touch, oral, and multisensory areas as measured by the *Sensory Profile* (Dunn, 1999). It is remarkable to find that more than 70% of these individuals experienced problems in modulation as it related to (a) movement affecting activity level, (b) sensory input affecting emotional responses, and (c) visual input affecting emotional responses, and activity level. Approximately two-thirds of children

---

Table 2.1

Characteristics of Asperger Syndrome

A. Qualitative impairment in social interaction, as manifested by at least two of the following:

(1) marked impairment in the use of multiple nonverbal behaviors such as eye-to-eye gaze, facial expression, body pressure, and gestures to regulate social interaction

(2) failure to develop peer relationships appropriate to developmental level

(3) a lack of spontaneous seeking to share enjoyment, interests, or achievements with other people (e.g., by a lack of showing, bringing, or pointing out objects of interest to other people)

(4) lack of social or emotional reciprocity

B. Restricted repetitive and stereotyped patterns of behavior, interests, and activities, as manifested by at least one of the following:

(1) encompassing preoccupation with one or more stereotyped and restricted patterns of interest that is abnormal either in intensity or focus

(2) apparently inflexible adherence to specific, nonfunctional routines or rituals

(3) stereotyped and repetitive motor mannerisms (e.g., hand or finger flapping or twisting, or complex whole-body movements)

(4) persistent preoccupation with parts of objects

C. The disturbance causes clinically significant impairment in social, occupational, or other important areas of functioning.

D. There is no clinically significant delay in language (e.g., single words used by age 2 years, communicative phrases used by 3 years).

E. There is no clinically significant delay in cognitive development or in the development of age-appropriate self-help skills, adaptive behavior (other than in social interaction), and curiosity about the environment in childhood.

F. Criteria are not met for another specific Pervasive Developmental Disorder or Schizophrenia.

From: *Diagnostic Criteria for Asperger's Disorder (299.80): The Diagnostic and Statistical Manual of Mental Disorders–Fourth Edition* (American Psychiatric Association, 1994).

Table 2.2
Definition of Asperger Syndrome

A disorder of uncertain nosological validity, characterized by the same kind of qualitative abnormalities of reciprocal social interaction that typify autism, together with a restricted, stereotyped repetitive repertoire of interests and activities. The disorder differs from autism primarily in that there is no general delay or retardation in language or cognitive development. Most individuals are of normal general intelligence, but it is common for them to be markedly clumsy; the condition occurs predominantly in boys (in a ratio of about eight boys to one girl). It seems highly likely that at least some cases represent mild varieties of autism, but it is uncertain whether or not that is so for all. There is a strong tendency for abnormalities to persist into adolescence and adult life, and it seems that they represent individual characteristics that are not greatly affected by environmental influences. Psychotic episodes occasionally occur in early adult life.

Diagnostic Guidelines

Diagnosis is based on the combination of a lack of any clinically significant general delay in language or cognitive development plus, as with autism, the presence of qualitative deficiencies in restricted, repetitive, stereotyped patterns of behavior, interests, and activities.

There may or may not be problems in communication similar to those associated with autism, but significant language retardation would rule out the diagnosis.

Includes: autistic psychopathy

schizoid disorder of childhood

Excludes: anankastic personality disorder (F60.5)

attachment disorders of childhood (F94.1, F94.2)

obsessive-compulsive disorder (F21)

schizotypal disorder (F21)

simple schizophrenia (F20.6)

From: *Asperger Syndrome Definition: The International Classification of Diseases and Related Health Problems–Tenth Edition* (World Health Organization, 1992).

and youth with AS in this sample evidenced emotional and social difficulties or problems related to their sensory processing. The majority of these individuals also had problems in all but one of the sensory factors identified by Dunn (1999). Table 2.3 gives an overview of the results of this study.

What follows is a brief description of the sensory areas as they relate to individuals with AS from the study by Myles and colleagues, the original work of Hans Asperger, and anecdotal reports of parents and teachers. Specifically, the following areas will be discussed: (a) tactile, (b) vestibular, (c) proprioception, (d) visual, (e) auditory, (f) gustatory, and (g) olfactory. The section concludes with a discussion of how sensory processing problems can impact the behavior and social/emotional states of individuals with AS.

Tactile

 Hans Asperger reported tactile problems in the children in his study. According to Asperger, "Many children have abnormally strong dislikes for particular tactile sensations, for example, velvet, silk, cotton, wool or chalk. They cannot tolerate the roughness of new shirts or of mended socks. Cutting fingernails is often the cause of tantrums" (p. 80).

Children with AS can be hypersensitive (overly sensitive) or hyposensitive (undersensitive) to tactile stimuli, falling anywhere along this continuum. Each of these states may bring with it a variety of problems that impact the individual with AS in a manner that can have a negative impact on school performance, friendships, social relationships, as well as home and community functioning.

Tactile Hypersensitivity

Asperger reported primarily on hypersensitive behaviors. Those who are hypersensitive feel actual physical discomfort when coming into contact with someone or something that the rest of us are barely aware of. Also known as *tactile defensiveness* (Ayres, 1979), hypersensitivity can impact all areas of functioning for individuals with AS.

Table 2.3

Sensory Profile Results

Sensory Characteristics	Definite Difference	Probable Difference	Typical Responses	No Response
Sensory Processing				
Auditory	57	29	12	2
Visual	19	19	45	14
Vestibular	48	7	31	14
Touch	56	29	4	10
Multisensory	50	36	12	2
Oral Sensory	31	19	24	26
Modulation				
Sensory Processing Related to Endurance/Tone	69	10	21	0
Modulation Related to Body Position and Movement	29	36	33	2
Modulation of Movement Affecting Activity Level	33	41	24	2
Modulation of Sensory Input Affecting Emotional Responses	71	17	12	0
Modulation of Visual Input Affecting Emotional Responses and Activity Level	33	48	17	2
Behavior and Emotional Responses				
Emotional/Social Responses	67	19	14	0
Behavioral Outcomes of Sensory Processing	78	10	10)	2
Items Indicating Thresholds for Response	21	31	46	2
***Sensory Profile* Factor Summary**				
Sensory Seeking	27	34	39	2
Emotionally Reactive	76	19	5	0
Low Endurance/Tone	71	10	19	0
Oral Sensory Sensitivity	76	0	0	24
Inattention/Distractibility	64	19	13	5
Poor Registration	59	17	17	7
Sensory Sensitivity	29	19	42	10
Sedentary	46	19	33	2
Fine/Motor Perceptual	35	10	50	5

Note. Percentages are presented.

At school, the child may scream when glue gets on her hands during an art project because of the way it feels, or she may refuse to help make the paper maché volcano during science for the same reason. Standing in line may also be a problem. Fearing that someone will come too close and touch her, Sarah, a child with AS, attempts to stand away from others or pushes somebody who comes too close. In return, other children may push back or attempt to ignore Sarah, whom they see as mean, thus impacting her social interactions with peers.*

At recess, tactile problems impact play choices. Mark is so hypersensitive to touch that he cannot stand to hold a baseball or football. In addition, he cannot tolerate standing too close to the children in his class. Therefore, he excludes himself from football, baseball, and any games that involve standing in a line (relay races, four-square) or in a group (red rover, freeze tag). Similarly, blowing bubbles, a common activity for young children, is uncomfortable for Mark and some children with AS who cannot stand the feel of the bubble soap on their hands or the way a bubble feels when it pops on their arm. For these reasons, a child with AS may not feel safe or comfortable in any of the activities that occur during recess. The end result – isolation.

Tactile hypersensitivity also impacts functioning at home. For example, children and youth who are hypersensitive may exclusively wear a certain type of fabric or tolerate clothes, only if they have been laundered in a specific detergent. Rachel's mother removes all of the tags from her daughter's clothing before she will wear them. She cannot just cut them out; she must remove the entire tag and the threads used to hold it in place. BJ only wears cotton sweatsuits from The Gap. His mother is not sure if it is the feel of the material, the pressure from the waist-band elastic, or the support from the neck or wrist bands that causes him to "feel right" when he wears these clothes. When asked, BJ can only say that his Gap sweatsuits feel right and that if he has to wear something else, he can't think.

---

*Often one behavior is caused by or related to more than one sensory processing area. For ease of understanding, each behavior is here attributed to the one sensory system that may often be the "culprit."

Personal hygiene may also be impacted. Hans Asperger noted that bath water provides unpleasant sensations to some. A washcloth can prove painful. Specific soaps seem abrasive. As a result, many hypersensitive children refuse to have their hair washed. John's dad reported his frustrations with John's hairwashing. John would cry and scream when it was time to wash his hair. His dad experimented with different types of shampoo, water temperature, water pressure, and ways to apply the shampoo. Finally he found that lukewarm water applied firmly with a washcloth was tolerable to John.

Eating is another problem for many children who are hypersensitive in the tactile area. Because of hypersensitivity, a child with AS may only eat certain textures of foods or meals served at a specific temperature. As a result, proper nutrition is often an issue. Luis will only eat crunchy foods, gagging when presented with foods that are soft or mushy. He doesn't appear to be sensitive to temperature, however, as he will eat most raw or partially cooked crisp vegetables and fruits (e.g., celery, carrots, broccoli, cauliflower, turnips, apples) and very crunchy peanut butter. He also likes to eat raw rice and pasta. Not surprisingly, he is a big fan of potato, sweet potato, and corn chips. Luis' mother, worried about his health, consulted with a nutritionist and an occupational therapist, who subsequently worked with her to make sure that Luis' diet contains all the necessary vitamins and minerals. These professionals also gave her ideas of how to meet her son's nutritional needs while slowly introducing new foods.

Tactile Hyposensitivity

As opposed to hypersensitive individuals, children and youth with AS who are hyposensitive may not feel or notice touch unless it is very firm or intense. Consequently, they are often slow to respond to or notice others who use touch to gain attention. Mrs. Johnson, a kindergarten general education teacher, was frustrated by Lin's lack of response. Mrs. Johnson often touched the children's shoulder to get their attention or to reinforce them. But Lin typically did not stop what she was doing or appeared not to notice that she was being touched. Mrs. Johnson thought Lin was ignoring her. It wasn't until she had a chance to talk to Lin's mother during parent-teacher conferences that Mrs. Johnson found out that Lin did not respond to light touch. Lin's mother also commented that Lin often seems to be unaware of scrapes or bruises from the playground on her arms and legs and does not know when or how they occurred.

Even though they may not respond to touch, some children with AS use touch to explore the environment. When the tactilely hyposensitive child is around, a teacher or parent often hears, "Gregory is touching me! Make him stop!" While standing in line at school or in the grocery store, Gregory touches the people in front of and behind him, as well as the objects in his vicinity. He is not trying to be annoying but uses touch to define where he is supposed to stand. He may stand too close to others with little or no regard for personal space. Asperger reported a similar profile in the children he studied, "For personal distance too they have no sense or feeling. Just as they unconcernedly lean on others, even complete strangers, and run their fingers over them as if they were a piece of furniture" (1944, p. 81).

Hyposensitivity may be accompanied by low muscle tone. As a result, many children with AS seem clumsy. They may sit half-on and half-off their chair, run into others, or trip over their own feet. They often have a weak grasp or tire easily during physical activities. Libby's father affectionately refers to his daughter as a truck. When Libby crosses the room, she steps on whatever is in her path and has trouble negotiating doorways. She often runs into door jams instead of passing cleanly through the door opening. Similarly, she cannot do sit-ups or push-ups and seems exhausted after attempting to play any physical sport.

Other children who are hyposensitive in the tactile area seek sensory sensations. For example, they hit or bite themselves when frustrated. Lance's nails are bitten down to the "quick" and often bleed. When he becomes upset, he presses his fingertips firmly into his desktop. The combination of raw fingertips pressed against a hard surface would be excruciating to most of us, but to Lance it feels good. Debbie, an occupational therapist, noticed that her son appeared to crave tactile input. He wears clothes that are too small or have tight elastic at the wrist, legs, and waist. Although her son often has indentations on his skin from the tight clothes, he never indicates any discomfort.

Vestibular

Approximately one half of the children and youth with AS studied by Myles and her colleagues (2000) experienced problems in the vestibular area. As stated in Chapter 1, the vestibular system is involved in movement, posture, vision, balance, and coordination of both sides of the body. As in the tactile area, individuals can be hypersensitive or hyposensitive relative to the vestibular system, and each type of sensitivity impacts functioning across home, school, and community.

Vestibular Hypersensitivity

Individuals with vestibular hypersensitivity tend to have a low tolerance for activities that involve movement. They also have difficulty changing direction and speed or maintaining a body position other than upright with feet on the floor. These individuals are called "gravitationally insecure" (Ayres, 1979) because of their fear of having their feet leave the ground. Some children with AS even lock their joints into a rigid position to stabilize their bodies.

Not surprisingly, these characteristics impact children's opportunities to participate in a variety of activities that sensory-typical children consider fun. Imagine a soccer game. It requires (a) running at inconsistent speeds; (b) constant position change while running down the field, looking at other players, following the ball; (c) quick movement to avoid players who may be after you; and (d) sometimes leaving the ground to reach for the ball. For a child with AS who experiences vestibular problems, soccer could be a nightmare. As a result, if encouraged to join a game of soccer by a well-meaning teacher or parent, the child might flatly refuse to play. If forced to participate, she might appear ill. When playing in general, the child likely would tire easily from running at a slow pace or would sit on the field. Most sports require intact vestibular systems (e.g., basketball, football, baseball). Often children with AS are not successful in these activities. Without being aware of the more scientific nature of their problems, peers may recognize the vestibular difficulties in children with AS who, consequently, are selected last when teams are created.

Like sports, gym can be a problematic time for children with AS.

Doing a somersault may be difficult, if not impossible. While the vestibularly hypersensitive child may attempt this activity, the fear of establishing a new position (particularly involving the head), the disorientation after moving into a crouching position, slowness in reorienting and pushing the body to do a somersault, combined with poor endurance would most likely make this another unsuccessful experience.

Some of the tasks required at school are also challenging for children who have this profile. For example, they may have difficulty copying from the board and lose their place on the page when reading. This often results in incomplete or sloppy work.

Home-based problems usually also exist. When trying to bend down and put her socks on, Margy often becomes distracted, overly excited or irritated. This is compounded by the tactile problems of having to wear the sock just right – so that the toe seam does not touch her toes. Her mother reports that meltdowns or tantrums were common in the morning before she talked with her child's occupational therapist. After confirming that Margy had vestibular issues, the occupational therapist and Margy's mother worked together to develop a wardrobe for Margy that did not (a) require pulling shirts over the head and (b) contain tight clothes that required twisting and pulling to put on. In addition, they placed Margy's clothes in a drawer at Margy's waist level so she did not need to bend down or reach over her head to get her clothes. These subtle changes have made a big difference in helping Margy begin the day on a positive note.

Individuals with vestibular hypersensitivity tend to have a low tolerance for activities that involve movement.

Playing board games is also a problem. The child with vestibular problems may move his entire body to look at another person during a game – not just his head. As a result, he may easily become tired. In addition, he may become distracted if he tries to attend to several children during a game – trying to move his entire body to listen to each child while taking a turn can be a great challenge.

Vestibular Hyposensitivity

Hyposensitivity is observed in the child who rocks back and forth in her chair or swings to the extent that we, as sensory-typical individuals, fear that she will become dizzy or nauseated. This child, too, might be clumsy and have difficulty starting and stopping activities that include movement. Jordan has to participate in relay races in gym class. He has voiced his dislike for the activity because he knows he cannot do it well but he has to do it anyway. When the whistle blows, he always is the last to begin. He runs slowly, his body seeming not to flow. In addition, he typically has trouble stopping at the finish line and often runs into other children.

His mother calls Sean a wiggle worm; his grandmother refers to him as a "bull in a china shop." Regardless of the term, Sean is in constant motion even when he is sitting. At the dinner table, he balances the chair on two legs, repositioning himself constantly. He is surrounded by chaos. His napkin drops to the floor. He drops his fork. When he leans over to pick it up, he nearly falls out of his chair. He drops the salt shaker; spills his milk. When he bends over to fix the mess, he often creates another. To avoid disaster, his grandmother attempts to "Sean-proof" her house before his visits by putting away all the knick-knacks and small treasures she has sitting around the house. Upon his arrival, Sean enters the house at full speed. He runs into his grandmother a bit too hard; she loses her balance but rights herself to return his hug. He then bumps into the end table; it falls over; Sean bends to pick it up. The rest of the visit is predictable – things fall to the ground; Sean is in constant motion. Although she loves him, Sean's grandmother heaves a sigh of relief when he leaves as she counts the broken figurines she had neglected to put away.

Proprioception

The muscles and joints send messages to help us move, sit, hold items, and balance. Thus, it is the proprioceptive system that allows us to sit down in a chair without looking and to know that we are pulling our shirt on correctly without watching ourselves in the mirror. This system also helps us keep our balance when walking; it helps us "right ourselves" when we are carrying heavy objects. Because of the proprioceptive system, we are able to perform activities without thinking about it. But for some children with AS, these movements are not automatic.

John has poor posture; he slumps. At school, he places his head in his hands when sitting at his desk. When he gets out of his chair, he uses his hand for stability and looks at his feet as if to ensure that they are doing the right thing. He ambles, rather than walks. He gets confused about right and left. When his teacher holds up a piece of paper and says, "Number starting here" and then points, John cannot find that specific place on his paper. He moves frequently, yet in a labored fashion, showing difficulty in "getting comfortable." Not surprisingly, gym is difficult for him. He can't follow directions to complete an obstacle course, nor can he follow the gym teacher's model when he is facing John. He avoids the jungle gym and bridge, because he cannot negotiate them.

At home, John has difficulty climbing stairs. He does it cautiously even though he has climbed the same steps for six years. Dressing is also a problem. John is slow – he has difficulty pulling a shirt over his head and finding the armholes. His mother has noticed that when he looks in the mirror to brush his teeth or comb his hair, he seems confused. He repositions his arms and hands or moves the hair or toothbrush. Sometimes while brushing his teeth he even misses his mouth.

John's mother thinks that he needs more sleep. He doesn't seem to have any energy. When asked to help clean the garage, he drops things, and when he attempts to pick up something that weighs just a few pounds, he complains that it is too heavy. After a few minutes of "work" in the garage, John complains of being tired – he even looks tired. Fatigue is also evident at dinner time; it seems to take John a lot of time and effort to do a simple task such as cutting his meat. After he has cut his meat, he is almost too tired to go on eating it. His dad watches him chew in a labored fashion. John is usually the last one to finish eating and his parents have to resist telling him to hurry up.

Visual

 Compared with other sensory areas, the visual system appears to be a relative strength for children and youth with AS. Myles and others (2000) found that almost one half of the 42 children they studied responded to visual input similarly to those who had no special needs. Less than 20% had definite visual-related problems; an additional 19% were likely to experience difficulties in this sensory area.

Visual problems related to sensory processing can take many forms. Often children and youth with AS cannot find what they are looking for. They appear not to see the social studies book in their desk that is "right there on top of the science book." They can't find the can of corn in the pantry that is "right before their eyes," or they don't see the green tee-shirt they are supposed to wear even though it is folded neatly in the dresser drawer.

However, these same children can find Charizard in a mess of 150 Pokemon™ cards. Why the discrepancy? Motivation and concentration may be the answers. It may take the child with AS tremendous concentration to focus on finding what he needs. When motivation is high, that concentration can be applied for short periods of time. But such concentration may be very tiring and require so much effort that it cannot be sustained easily for long periods of time.

Many children have writing problems that may, in part, be visually based. Their writing appears sloppy. Even when copying from the board or from a model on their desk, they have difficulty staying on the line or maintaining appropriate spacing between letters. They may erase often in an attempt to conform to conventional writing standards. Further, frequently their performance on writing tasks does not match what they seem to know. Zachary has an IQ of 144 and is extremely verbal on most topics and can spell orally almost any word in the dictionary. However, when asked to write his spelling words, he tends to make mistakes. His average grade on a written spelling test is 40%, while his accuracy rate on oral spelling test exceeds 90%.

Zach's handwriting is also an anomaly. His obsession is Star Trek and he has filled notebooks with his adventures as a member of the Enterprise crew. In addition, using drawings and text, he has designed a "better and more efficient Star Ship Enterprise." Why the discrepancy between spelling performance and Star Trek writings? There are many possible reasons. Motivation is an obvious answer. Pacing is another. When writing about Star Trek, Zach chooses when and how much to write. If he is tired or stressed, he may write very little in one setting. If everyone in the house is quiet and he has had a relatively successful school day, he may write for a long time. His concentration to task on Star Trek is different than for spelling. He knows the Star Trek information and it comes easily, so his only effort is the writing task. However, to spell correctly he must concentrate on *both* the writing and the content. Thus, writing on a spelling test presents more of a cognitive drain.

Children with AS may also have visual oversensitivities.

Children with AS may also have visual oversensitivities that are difficult for others to comprehend. For example, Nicole cannot concentrate or work in a room that has fluorescent lighting. She says that she can see the light pulsating and that the movement is very disrupting and hurts her eyes. Jonathan loves being read to but he does not like to read himself because he says it is too hard. When you see Jonathan read, his problems become apparent. He skips lines and words and moves his head from side to side to follow the text. Even when he uses his finger to keep his place, he does not read smoothly or evenly.

Auditory

Meara (1999) found that children with AS do not process auditory information the same way as their nondisabled peers. Myles and her colleagues' results confirm that observation, as over 85% of the children they studied had definite or probable auditory problems. The identified problems were related to auditory processing rather than traditional hearing problems. That is, these children typically have intact hearing abilities; however, they may not efficiently or accurately interpret auditory information.

Children and youth with AS may be hyper- and/or hyposensitive to noise. It is possible that they are at both ends of the continuum depending on the type of stimuli they are trying to process. Summarizing his case studies of individuals with autistic psychopathy, Hans Asperger wrote, "There is hypersensitivity too against noise. Yet the same children who are distinctly hypersensitive to noise in particular situations, in other situations may appear to be hyposensitive. They may appear to be switched off even to loud noises" (1944, p. 80).

Auditory Hypersensitivity

Some children with AS respond negatively to loud noises. As a result, fire drills are often painful. Trevor's parents reported that the fire drill noise is so painful to him that he screams and cries when it occurs. In fact, the very thought of a fire drill drives Trevor to distraction. He obsesses so much about the possibility that a fire drill will take place that he maintains a high level of stress and anxiety as a result of his "fright, flight, fight" response, leaving him unable to concentrate on little else. In the state where he lives, October is fire drill month and unannounced fire drills occur at frequent intervals. During the entire month, Trevor asks his teacher incessantly about fire drills. His anxiety level is so high that relatively small events such as schedule changes or not being able to be first in line cause full-blown meltdowns. At home Trevor is in tears constantly and all he can talk about is the fire drill. It is so bad that his parents have discussed with his school-based team the possibility of home schooling during the month of October.

Even small noises can be irritating to individuals with AS. Mica hears the brushing sound of corduroy when her classmates wear clothing made of this material. When this happens, she can concentrate on nothing else. The sound of a violin is painful to Jack, who refuses to attend school assemblies that feature an orchestra or attend the symphony with his parents. McKenzie cannot tolerate the sound of a metal fork scraping a glass plate. As a result, if her parents or sister accidentally make this sound while eating, McKenzie flies into a rage and covers her ears ("fright, flight, fight").

Some children cannot concentrate in the presence of noise. Background noise simply stops them from working. They cannot listen to someone talk with the television on. In class, if other children are talking or even whispering, a child with AS may not be able to read or complete a worksheet. Michael's teacher noticed that when the class was taking a spelling test, he would stand his folders and notebooks up around him, seemingly trying to block out others around him. When she asked him why he did this, he told her that he could not concentrate with all of the noise around him. Yet, to Michael's teacher, the class seemed quiet.

Auditory Hyposensitivity

Parents and teachers often report that their children and students do not respond to them, even when there is no background noise. Sixty-three percent of teachers and parents surveyed about their children with AS responded that their children did not appear to hear what they said to them. Over one half indicated that individuals with AS did not respond when their names were called.

Hyposensitivity is also seen in the child who seems oblivious to everything going on around him. Mr. Higgins reported that sometimes Jonathan sits in his seventh-grade classroom staring into space. Even during cooperative groups, Jonathan may be there physically but mentally he appears to be elsewhere. Mr. Higgins has asked Jonathan numerous times what he is thinking about, but Jonathan always replies, "Nothing." Mr. Higgins suspects that Jonathan is deep in thought about his latest obsession – atomic power.

Melanie reports that her daughter acts in a similar manner. She may be in conversation with someone and then suddenly drift away. One time her daughter, Julie, and a friend were discussing baseball. When the friend mentioned something about bats, Julie replied, "Albino bats" and promptly became silent. Her friend continued to talk about baseball, but Julie didn't seem to hear. Her mother knew that she was "off somewhere" thinking about the nocturnal mammals.

Gustatory

 The gustatory or sense of taste can also be a problem area for children and youth with AS. An analysis of items on the *Sensory Profile* in the study by Myles et al. (2000) revealed that more than one third of the individuals with AS (a) avoided certain tastes that are typical of children's diets, (b) would only eat foods with certain tastes, and/or (c) were picky eaters. Asperger in his work found similar characteristics, "There is often a preference for very sour or strongly spiced food, such as gherkins or roast meat. Often there is an insurmountable dislike of vegetables or dairy product" (1944, p. 80).

Proper nutrition is always a concern when individuals do not eat a wide variety of food. George, at age nine, only eats chicken fingers, chicken fried steak, and potato chips. His mother has worked with a multidisciplinary team that included a nutritionist and an occupational therapist to ensure that her son gets the nutrients he needs and to develop a plan to gradually introduce new foods in George's diet.

Cynda's mother had a very difficult time with her daughter getting ready for school. It seemed that every morning started on the wrong foot, with Cynda requiring constant reminders to keep to the task of getting ready. The biggest battle occurred when it was time for Cynda to brush her teeth. In frustration, Cynda's mother told her neighbor, an early childhood special educator with an occupational therapy background, about the stressful mornings she and her daughter experienced. The neighbor, who happened to be on maternity leave, volunteered to come to Cynda's home and witness the morning "routine." As she watched Cynda begrudgingly get ready despite constant prompts from her mother, she saw no unusual behaviors until it came to toothbrushing. Cynda had to be almost physically moved into the bathroom where her mother put toothpaste on the toothbrush as Cynda whined. As Cynda's mother put the toothbrush up to Cynda's mouth, Cynda gagged. The neighbor suggested that Cynda not brush her teeth that morning and go on to school. Later in the day, the neighbor and Cynda's mother discussed the possibility that the mere thought of the taste of the toothpaste might be causing the morning routine to go awry. When she learned that Cynda was a picky eater, the neighbor suggested that Cynda's mother talk with Cynda about the toothpaste to find out if it was the taste that was the trouble.

Olfactory

Over 75% of the children with AS who participated in Myles and her colleagues' study were considered to have oral sensory sensitivity. The olfactory or sense of smell is categorized as a type of oral sensory sensitivity. When asked specifically whether their children avoided certain smells that are a typical part of the environment, 40% of parents and teachers responded affirmatively. So it appears that "smell" is a problem area for many children and youth with AS.

Our olfactory system is constantly bombarded with smells. In fact, most of us are unaware of the extent to which smells exist in the environment. The child with AS who has a sensitivity in this area has many diverse smells to deal with. At school, there are smells associated with (a) the teachers' and students' aftershave or cologne; (b) fluids used to clean the blackboard and floors; (c) glue, paste, paints, and other art supplies; (d) cafeteria food; and (e) gym or physical education locker rooms. In addition, for the child who is extremely sensitive to smell, the unique body odor that each of us possesses can be problematic.

At home, various smells from the following are present: (a) cooking; (b) cleaning supplies used to dust, mop, and polish windows; (c) soaps, shampoos, and conditioners used in bathing; (d) makeup, per-fumes, aftershaves, and colognes used by family members; (e) fire burning in the fireplace; and (f) pet-related odors. The community is even more replete with smells; for example, each store has its own par-ticular set of smells – some pleasant like the local bagel store; some not-so-pleasant like the paint section in the hardware store.

Every time Elise took her daughter Ivory to the grocery store, some sort of "battle" ensued, with Ivory complaining incessantly as they walked down the aisles. Her complaints were generally global, typi-cal teenager complaints such as, "I hate grocery shopping," "This is so stupid," "Why do I have to go with you?" Elise came to dread having Ivory with her at the grocery store. Likewise, Ivory wanted nothing more than not to go with her mother to the store. One evening as they were watching television, Elise asked her daughter why she didn't like going to the grocery store. After wading through the teenager remarks, Elise finally heard the real reason for the protest – the grocery store smelled bad or in Ivory's words, "It smells gross. Worse than the perfume you used to wear."

On the next grocery trip, Elise went alone. She made an effort to attend to all of the different smells and found that there were indeed many smells – each section had its own scent that often combined in a not-so-pleasing manner. Elise spoke with the multidisciplinary school team about Ivory's sensitivity to smell at her Individualized Education Plan (IEP) meeting. The occupational therapist told her that some chil-dren with AS, like Ivory, have problems processing olfactory informa-tion that could lead to a "fright, flight, fight" response. She provided Elise with some strategies to help Ivory become less sensitive to smell. Her first recommendation, however, was to consider going grocery shopping by herself for a while.

Behavioral and Emotional Responses to Sensory Stimuli

The sensory system has a tremendous and often negative impact on the behavior of children and youth with AS. In fact, parents' respons-es to items under this category on the *Sensory Profile* (Dunn, 1999) indicated that this is the greatest area of concern for children and youth with AS (Myles et al., 2000). As shown in Table 2.4, a substantial number of children and youth with AS frequently or always:

- seem anxious
- display emotional outbursts when unsuccessful
- demonstrate poor frustration tolerance
- are sensitive to criticism
- cry easily

In addition, they:

- don't tolerate change in plans, expectations, and routines
- are inefficient at accomplishing tasks
- don't perceive body language and expressions correctly.

Parents and teachers also report that these children:

- have trouble growing up
- have difficulty making friends
- need more protection from life's events than do others.

Based on these findings, a picture of the child with AS emerges. This is a child who, although working hard, may not complete his work. He can't tell whether his teachers are pleased with him or upset with him. When changes occur in his environment, his already anxious state intensifies, leading him to cry, scream, or tantrum to express his frustration – or to "withdraw." He wants to have friends, but he doesn't understand their social language. In this intense emotional state he may demonstrate behaviors or coping strategies that are more typical of younger children since they are most familiar and may have been successful in the past. He is extremely gullible with peers, particularly those who have recognized a potential vulnerability. This may lead to bullying, teasing or practical jokes to elicit what is perceived as a humorous or entertaining reaction. Such peers can lead him along to break rules as he does not understand the social ramifications. Additionally, his interpretation of their behaviors is that this is what friends do when they are together.

Now factor sensory issues into this picture. He has *tactile* problems. He doesn't understand the concept of space and feels uncomfortable standing in lines or being too close to others. This creates anxiety. He

Table 2.4
Emotional/Social Concerns
Identified by Parents and Teachers of
Children with Asperger Syndrome

Sensory Profile Item	Response
Emotional Responses	
Expresses feeling like a failure	31
Doesn't express emotions	33
Cries easily	34
Is stubborn or uncooperative	47
Is sensitive to criticism	50
Seems anxious	62
Displays emotional outbursts when unsuccessful at a task	66
Has poor frustration tolerance	71
Social Issues	
Seems to have difficulty liking self	34
Doesn't perceive body language or facial expressions	42
Has definite fears	55
Needs more protection from life than other children	62
Has trouble "growing up"	66
Has difficulty making friends	80
Flexibility and Efficiency	
Uses inefficient ways of doing things	48
Has difficulty tolerating changes in routine	59
Has difficulty tolerating changes in plans and expectations	69

Note. "Response" means percent of parents and teachers who reported that the child with Asperger Syndrome always and frequently had problems in these areas.

has problems writing. In addition to fine-motor problems, the sound of the pencil writing on paper is grating to him. *Vestibular* problems are also evident. He has difficulty copying from the chalkboard and he is fatigued because in order to face someone, he needs to move his entire body toward them and concentrate – hard. The *proprioceptive* system also causes difficulties. He always wants to do his work in the bean bag chair at the back of the room, but since there is only one, it is not always available. He can't seem to concentrate unless he is in the bean bag chair or lying on the floor. He has *auditory* problems and doesn't process what the teachers say or does so very slowly. He may not respond right on time or do what he is supposed to do. Yet, when asked to repeat back what was said, he may be able to do it verbatim. When his teacher makes a comment about his attention, he is not sure what she meant. Was she upset, was she teasing? He is constantly on the alert for a noise that is painful for him – he fears the fire alarm and the static noise made by the intercom system before an announcement. To cope, he sometimes tunes it out. He seems oblivious to everything going on around him. When his teacher gets his attention, he doesn't know how long he was "gone" or what he missed. He also doesn't know how to get the information he missed in the meantime. His *visual* sense may be the strongest, but he may still have trouble finding the social studies book in his desk. He may also have difficulty concentrating if the lights are too bright or too dim.

Finally, add in *gustatory* and *olfactory* problems. He is particularly stressed by gym and lunch, which occur right after one another. Gym is a problem because of all the smells. Just thinking about them upsets the child with AS. Lunch is another challenge. He forgot his sack lunch and the food in the lunchroom tastes like sandpaper; the smell of the lunchroom is even worse. He is hungry but knows that the food will likely make him gag. What can he do to get food that he likes?

If you were the child with AS and had some or all of these problems, how would you act or react? How long would it take before you exploded? Or withdrew? Considering how much children and youth with AS have to tolerate on a daily basis, it is no wonder they sometimes resort to tantrums, rage or meltdowns. But as we will see in Chapter 4, we can help restructure their environment to reduce or eliminate sensory issues.

Chapter 3

ASSESSING SENSORY PROCESSING ISSUES

Children and youth with Asperger Syndrome (AS) display a variety of complex behaviors across academic, behavioral, social/emotional, leisure/recreational, and vocational areas. Each of these areas may be impacted by sensory processing issues. As we have seen in the previous chapters, sensory problems are variable and can occur inconsistently, interfering with performance at home, school, and community. To challenge those of us who live or work with these children even more, these behaviors can be sporadic, occurring on one occasion and not on another even when the circumstances appear to be identical. Sensory difficulties can be impacted by a variety of variables that may include:

- amount of structure present
- task requirements
- adult personality involved
- level of stress of the person with AS
- changes in routine
- method of instructional delivery
- amount of rest
- level of abstraction

Additional variables may be specific to individuals or the situations in which they are involved. To determine possible causes and solutions to these otherwise puzzling behaviors and reactions, teachers and parents must become "sensory detectives" (see Figure 3.1).

All of these variables make the assessment of sensory issues challenging. Simply using one checklist for one observation in one environment may not yield accurate information. In order to develop inter-

Figure 3.1. Sensory detective at work.

vention strategies that will support the child across various settings and situations at home and at school, we must try to understand the behaviors we observe. Accurate and effective assessment of an individual's sensory needs requires thorough examination of the child and her environments. Table 3.1 lists several considerations that can support effective assessment. We realize that time constraints and staff availability may preclude you from addressing each of these considerations. Collaboration among various adults in the child's many environments is one way to address assessment in a more timely fashion.

In this chapter we will review several tools currently used by professionals to gather information about sensory-related behaviors. In addition, issues involved in interpretation are discussed.

Table 3.1

Techniques and Suggestions
for Evaluating Individuals with Autism

---

1. Assess individuals across a variety of settings (e.g., recess, music, social studies, lunchroom). A series of brief assessments that represent students' environments is preferred to one lengthy observation in one environment.

2. Observe students in the presence of different individuals (e.g., teachers, peers, parent).

3. Examine student behavior under varied task demands (i.e., independent activities, written work, group work, unstructured activities).

4. Observe students at different times of the day (i.e., morning, afternoon, before or after lunch).

5. Seek information from multiple respondents (i.e., teachers, parents, paraprofessionals, ancillary staff, peers).

6. If possible, assess students in a variety of potentially stress-invoking scenarios (i.e., an unexpected change in routine, instruction with a high level of verbal content, academic demands above instructional level, presence of a substitute teacher).

7. Consider the environmental or assessment setting as a critical component for understanding the student's behavior (i.e., proximity of student to teacher, desk arrangement, lighting, noise levels).

8. Talk to the student. Some insights may be gleaned by just asking the right questions.

9. Consider the value of observation during other assessments. Observing the student during intelligence or achievement testing can provide valuable insights and assist in selecting the appropriate sensory assessment.

10. Look for patterns as well as differences of performance across multiple variables. These can provide valuable insights for developing interventions.

Adapted from Lowrence, L. (1994). *Techniques and suggestions for evaluating persons with autism.* Paper presented at the meeting of the Autism Society of America Convention Kansas City, MO.

Assessment Tools

Keep in mind that we are attempting to look at behaviors from a sensory processing perspective. Although neuroscientists are learning more and more about sensory processing and behavior, we are not yet able to determine definitive cause-effect relationships. Current "best practice" in assessment techniques reflects this growing knowledge in the neurosciences and its application to sensory processing in everyday life.

A variety of instruments exist that provide valuable information about sensory processing. These measures can be categorized as formal and informal. Formal assessments include norm-referenced and standardized instruments that compare an individual's profile to those of typically developing peers. Informal assessments, on the other hand, consist of reviews of records, inventories/checklists, interviews, and observations. Informal assessments often provide descriptive information about behaviors and can be useful in developing strategies that address those behaviors. However, they do not yield developmental scores for comparison with a normative population. Unlike most formal assessments, informal tools are usually easy to administer, are inexpensive, and do not require specific training to be conducted. Occupational therapists typically have a foundation of understanding about sensory processing and can administer and interpret sensory processing assessments.

Formal Assessments

Three formal assessments are summarized here: (a) the *Sensory Profile* (Dunn, 1999); (b) the *Short Sensory Profile* (Dunn, 1999); and (c) *Sensory Integration and Praxis Test* (SIPT) (Ayres, 1989). Table 3.2 overviews these measures.

Sensory Profile **(Dunn, 1999).** This 125-item norm-referenced questionnaire can be completed by someone who is very familiar with the child. This may include, but is not limited to, parents, teachers, paraprofessionals, therapists and childcare providers. The items on the profile describe children's behavioral responses to different sensory experiences, such as their reactions to specific sensory stimuli (auditory/visual/vestibular, etc.) and their ability to modulate their reac-

Table 3.2
Formal Assessment Measures

Title	Author	Year	Administration Time	Age Range	Who Can Complete the Tool	Who Can Score/ Interpret the Tool
Sensory Profile	Dunn	1999	30 min	5-11 yrs (also includes information on 3- and 4-year-olds)	Parents, teachers, others familiar with child	OTs, professionals with a strong foundation in sensory integration and sensory processing theory
Short Sensory Profile	Dunn	1999	10-15 minutes	3-17 yrs	Parents, teachers, others very familiar with child	OTs, professionals with a strong foundation in sensory integration and sensory processing theory
Sensory Integration and Praxis Test	Ayres	1989	10 min per subtest; all 17 subtests at least 10 min	4-8.11 yrs	Professionals trained and certified through Sensory Integration International or Western Psychological Services	Tests must be submitted to publisher for scoring or be scored on presold computer disks. Interpretation is included with scores

Note. OT=occupational therapist.

47

tions efficiently. In addition, the *Sensory Profile* provides a description of emotional and behavioral responses associated with sensory processing difficulties. Example of items from the three main categories of the profile are shown in Figure 3.2.

The *Sensory Profile* can be given in an interview format that allows for clarification of the items if requested. It can also be given or mailed to the respondent for completion. The person completing the profile reads each description and determines how often the child engages in the behavior *(always, frequently, occasionally, seldom, or never)*. This portion of the profile takes approximately 30 minutes to complete. The responses are then scored so that the results can be compared to a normative sample of children without disabilities. In the manual Dunn provides comparison profiles for three- and four-year-old children to illustrate developmentally appropriate performance for these ages.

Scores are classified as being within a *Typical Performance, Probable Difference*, or *Definite Difference* range. Scores falling in the *Probable Difference* and *Definite Difference* ranges are indicative of challenges in the child's ability to process sensory input and modulate or regulate her responses to sensory input. To interpret profile results and subsequently plan effective intervention strategies requires a solid understanding of sensory processing and how it can affect a child's ability to participate in home and school activities. Scoring and interpretation of the profile usually takes approximately 20 to 30 minutes.

***Short Sensory Profile* (Dunn, 1999).** This abbreviated 38-item form of the *Sensory Profile*, researched by McIntosh, Miller, Shyu and Dunn, is appropriate for children aged 3 to 17. It can be used as a screening tool to determine whether or not more indepth sensory assessment is needed. The profile can be administered in about 10 minutes and scored and interpreted in 10 to 20 minutes.

***Sensory Integration and Praxis Test (SIPT)* (Ayres, 1989).** This standardized battery of 17 tests is designed to identify patterns of function and dysfunction in sensory integration and motor planning (praxis). Appropriate for children aged 4 through 8 years, 11 months of age, administration of this assessment tool is time-consuming (2 hours) although any of the individual tests can be administered separately in approximately 10 minutes. The publisher specifies that any combination of tests can be used and scored. Therefore, it is not nec-

---

Sensory Profile

Sensory Processing:

Auditory Processing
> Responds negatively to unexpected or loud noises
> Doesn't respond when name is called (hearing is ok)

Visual Processing
> Covers eyes or squints to protect eyes from light
> Becomes frustrated when trying to find objects in competing backgrounds

Vestibular Processing
> Becomes anxious or distressed when feet leave the ground
> Seeks all kinds of movement activities

Touch Processing
> Expresses distress during grooming
> Touches people and objects to the point of irritating others

Multisensory Processing
> Has difficulty paying attention
> Leaves clothes twisted on body

Oral Sensory Processing
> Shows strong preference for certain tastes
> Mouths objects

Modulation:

Sensory Processing Related to Endurance/Tone
> Has a weak grasp
> Props to support self

Modulation Related to Body Position and Movement
> Seems accident-prone
> Takes movement or climbing risks during play that compromise safety

Modulation of Movement Affecting Activity Level
> Prefers quiet sedentary play
> "On the go"

Modulation of Sensory Input Affecting Emotional Responses
> Rigid rituals in personal hygiene
> Doesn't perceive body language or facial expressions

Modulation of Visual Input Affecting Emotional Responses and Activity Level
> Avoids eye contact
> Watches everyone when they move around the room

Figure 3.2. Sample items across the three main sections of the *Sensory Profile* (Dunn, 1999).

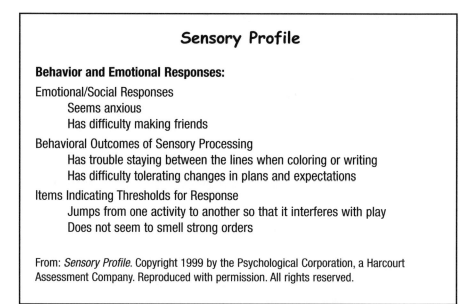

Figure 3.2. *(continued)*

essary to complete all 17 tests. Items are either observation- or performance-based. Tests may be computer scored by mailing protocols to the publisher or by using a computer program. Competent administration and interpretation of this assessment measure requires specific training and certification provided by Sensory Integration International or Western Psychological Services.

Informal Assessments

Six informal measures are also summarized in this section: (a) *Sensory Integration Inventory-Revised* (Reisman & Hanschu, 1992); (b) *Checklist for Occupational Therapy* (Occupational Therapy Associates-Watertown, 1997); (c) *Building Bridges Through Sensory Integration* (Yack, Sutton, & Aquilla, 1998); (d) *Questions to Guide Classroom Observations* (Kientz & Miller, 1999); and (e) *Motivation Assessment Scale* (Durand & Crimmins, 1992). Table 3.3 overviews these measures.

Sensory Integration Inventory-Revised (SII-R) (Reisman & Hanschu, 1992). This screening tool can be used in two ways: (a) it can be completed in approximately 30 minutes by therapists or teach-

Table 3.3
Informal Assessment Measures

Title	Author	Year	Administration Time	Age Range	Who Can Complete the Tool	Who Can Score/ Interpret the Tool
Sensory Integration Profile-Revised	Reisman & Hanschu	1992	30 min	Children and adults	Parents, teachers, others familiar with child	Professionals trained in SI, OTs, PTs, others
Checklist of Occupational Therapy	Occupational Therapy Associates-Watertown	1997	NS: Less than 20 min	Infants through adults (four scales)	Teachers, OTs, PTs, speech-language pathologists, team members	Professionals trained in SI, OTs, PTs, others
Building Bridges Through Sensory Integration	Yack, Sutton, & Aquilla	1998	NS: 20-45 min	NS	Parents, teachers, others familiar with child	Professionals trained in SI, OTs, PTs, others
Indicators of Sensory Processing Difficulties	Abrash	n.d.	NS: 10-15 min	NS	Parents, teachers, others familiar with child	Professionals trained in SI, OTs, PTs, others
Questions to Guide Classroom Observations	Kientz & Miller	1999	Minimum 1-3 hr on separate occasions	NS	Parents, teachers, others familiar with child	Professionals trained in SI, OTs, PTs, others
Motivation Assessment Guide	Durand & Crimmins	1992	NS: 10-15 min	NS	Parents, teachers, others familiar with child	Professionals familiar with tool

Note. NS=not specified; OT=occupational therapist; PT=physical therapist; SI=sensory integration.

ers familiar with a child, or (b) it can be used by an occupational therapist as a semi-structured interview for parents, teachers, caretakers, and others. Respondents mark whether or not a described behavioral response is *typical, not typical,* or *don't know.* Inventory items are considered to reflect possible patterns of sensory processing difficulties and, therefore, are organized into four sections: tactile, vestibular, proprioceptive, and general reactions. Subheadings within each section contain clusters of related items. The items are not converted to numeric ratings for a scale but are considered together for interpretation by a therapist. According to the authors, this tool is appropriate for children and adults with developmental disabilities and intellectual impairments. Table 3.4 provides a list of the areas assessed in this instrument.

Bonnie Hanschu, one of the authors of the SII-R, has developed a scoring grid, *Ready Approach – Key for Interpreting the Sensory Integration Inventory for Individuals with Developmental Disabilities* (Hanshu, 1998). This can help determine whether or not the observed behaviors are indicative of sensory defensiveness, sensory modulation difficulties, sensory registration difficulties, or sensory integration difficulties. The grid provides specific intervention protocols or strategies based on which area is most evident.

Checklist for Occupational Therapy **(Occupational Therapy Associates-Watertown, 1997).** This series of four checklists for infants, preschool-age children, school-age children, and adolescents-adults provides information about certain behaviors and whether they are seen frequently or not. The items look at behaviors that can be related to sensory processing difficulties (movement, sound, sight, self-regulation, touch), with categories of behaviors changing across the age ranges. The infant-through-school-age checklists ask whether a behavior occurs frequently or not, whereas the adolescent-adult checklist can be rated on a 1 to 5 scale with 1 being *never* and 5 *always.* According to the authors, the instrument can be completed by teachers, daycare providers, occupational therapists or physical therapists without specific prior training (see Figure 3.3).

Building Bridges Through Sensory Integration **(Yack et al., 1998).** This screening instrument asks respondents to consider a child's behaviors across sensory areas (vestibular, tactile, proprioceptive, visual, auditory, and olfactory/gustatory) within the context of specific daily tasks such as general self-care, dressing, eating, school/work, play and social interaction tasks. Responses provide valuable clues to sensory processing issues. The instrument is teacher- and parent-friendly, completed by checking whether specific behaviors are observed in the child. Responses can be used to develop inter-

---

Table 3.4
Sections on the Sensory Integration Inventory – Revised (Reisman & Hanschu, 1992)

Tactile
  Dressing
  Other Activities of Daily Living
  Personal Space
  Social
  Self-Stimulatory Behaviors
  Self-Injurious Behaviors

Vestibular
  Muscle Tone
  Equilibrium Responses
  Posture and Movement
  Bilateral Coordination
  Spatial Perception
  Emotional Expression
  Self-Stimulatory Behaviors

Proprioception
  Muscle Tone
  Motor Skills/Planning and Body Image
  Self-Stimulatory Behaviors
  Self-Injurious Behaviors

General Reactions
  (This section has no subheadings. Nine items are included.)

Note. Each subheading within each section includes a "comments" space for the reporter. Information about whether the indicators on the inventory are long-standing or of recent onset is solicited from the reporter.

Does child exhibit the following behaviors?	Yes, frequently	Sometimes	Never	Comments
GROSS-MOTOR SKILLS				
1. Seems weaker or tires more easily than other children his/her age.				
2. Difficulty with hopping, jumping, skipping, or running compared to other his/her age.				
3. Appears stiff and awkward in movements.				
4. Clumsy or seems not to know how to move body; bumps into things.				
5. Tendency to confuse right and left body sides.				
6. Hesitates to climb or play on playground equipment.				
7. Reluctant to participate in sports or physical activity; prefers table activities.				
8. Seems to have difficulty learning new motor tasks.				
9. Difficulty pumping self on swing; poor skills in rhythmic clapping games.				
FINE-MOTOR SKILLS				
1. Poor desk posture (slumps, leans on arm, head too close to work, other hand does not assist).				
2. Difficulty drawing, coloring, copying, cutting; avoidance of these activities.				
3. Poor pencil grasp; drops pencil frequently.				
4. Pencil lines are tight, wobbly, too faint or too dark; breaks pencil more often than usual.				
5. Tight pencil grasp; fatigues quickly in writing or other pencil and paper tasks.				

Figure 3.3. Sample items from *School-Age Checklist for Occupational Therapy, Ages 5-12 Years* (Occupational Therapy Associates-Watertown, 1997).

TOUCH	Yes, frequently	Sometimes	Never	Comments
1. Seems oversensitive to being touched; pulls away from light touch.				
2. Has trouble keeping hands to self, will poke or push other children.				
3. Touches things constantly; "learns" through his/her fingers.				
4. Has trouble controlling his interactions in group games such as tag, dodge ball.				
5. Avoids putting hands on messy substances (clay, finger paint, paste).				
6. Seems to be unaware of being touched or bumped.				
7. Has trouble remaining in busy or group situations, i.e., cafeteria, circle time.				
MOVEMENT AND BALANCE				
1. Fearful of moving through space (teeter-totter, swing).				
2. Avoids activities that challenge balance; poor balance in motor activities.				
3. Seeks quantities of movement including swinging, spinning, bouncing, and jumping.				
4. Difficulty or hesitance learning to climb or descend stairs.				
5. Seems to fall frequently.				
6. Gets nauseated or vomits from other movement experiences, e.g., swings, playground merry-go-rounds.				
7. Appears to be in constant motion, unable to sit still during an activity.				
VISUAL PERCEPTION				
1. Difficulty naming or matching colors, shapes, or sizes.				
2. Difficulty in completing puzzles; trial and error placement of pieces.				

From: *School-Age Checklist for Occupational Therapy, Ages 5-12 Years.* Used with permission by Occupational Therapy Associates-Watertown, 124 Watertown St., Watertown, MA 02172.

Figure 3.3. *(continued)*

vention strategies that can be used throughout the day to address the sensory issues identified (see Figure 3.4).

Indicators of Sensory Processing Difficulties **(Abrash, n.d.).** Respondents who complete this checklist are requested to place a mark beside observed behaviors across several sensory and regulatory areas including tactile, proprioception, vision, auditory, gustatory (taste), olfactory (smell), vestibular/kinesthetic, chemical regulation, arousal, and attending and social consciousness. In addition, behaviors in the tactile and vestibular/kinesthetic areas are divided into hypo- and hyperreactive. Similarly, vision behaviors are divided into acuity and oculomotor function, visual perception, and hyperreactivity. Following completion of this checklist, a determination can be made by an occupational therapist or related professional as to whether or not to pursue further observation and/or assessment. Information gleaned from the checklist can also serve as a catalyst for discussion between the therapist and teacher as a way of arriving at basic interventions that can be implemented in the classroom.

Questions to Guide Classroom Observation **(Kientz & Miller, 1999).** This tool, shown in Table 3.5, provides a format to guide teachers, therapists, or others familiar with sensory processing in observing a child in the classroom setting. A series of 38 questions address the following areas: (a) child, (b) task, (c) physical environment, (d) social context, and (e) cultural context. The questions are designed to help the observer analyze the child's behavior, the tasks in which she participates, and the environment in which she is asked to perform. Results of this observational assessment can yield information about sensory processing and its impact on a child's ability to perform expected activities in the classroom. It is most often used in conjunction with other formal or informal measures.

Motivation Assessment Scale **(Durand & Crimmins, 1992).** This scale can be useful in determining whether or not a specific behavior has a sensory function or cause. The authors developed the *Motivation Assessment Scale* on the premise that all behavior serves to communicate and is purposeful. It is up to those who live and work with a child to determine his or her communicative intent in a given situation.

Sensory Screening

Vestibular System

Does your child:
- ❏ Appear fearful of playground equipment or carnival rides.
- ❏ Become sick easily in cars, elevators, rides.
- ❏ Appear fearful of heights or stair climbing.
- ❏ Avoid balancing activities.
- ❏ Seek fast-moving activities.
- ❏ Avoid participation in sports or active games.
- ❏ Seem oblivious to risks of heights and moving equipment.
- ❏ Engage in frequent spinning, jumping, bouncing, running.

Tactile System

Does your child:
- ❏ Avoid touch or contact.
- ❏ Dislike and avoid messy play.
- ❏ Appear irritated by certain clothing and food textures.
- ❏ Appear irritated when someone is in close proximity.
- ❏ Often appear very active or fidgety.
- ❏ Have difficulty manipulating small objects.
- ❏ Use their hands to explore objects.
- ❏ Mouth objects.

Proprioceptive System

Does your child:
- ❏ Exert too much or not enough pressure while handling objects.
- ❏ Assume body positions necessary to perform different tasks.
- ❏ Enjoy rough and tumble play.
- ❏ Seek deep pressure by squeezing between furniture.
- ❏ Relax when given firm massages.

Visual System

Does your child:
- ❏ Appear uncomfortable in strong sunlight.
- ❏ Appear sensitive to changes in lighting.
- ❏ Turn away from television or computer screens.
- ❏ Focus on shadows, reflections, spinning objects.
- ❏ Have difficulty scanning environment.
- ❏ Respond when new people enter a room.

Auditory System

Does your child:
- ❏ Become upset with loud or unexpected noises.
- ❏ Hum or sing to screen out unwanted noise.
- ❏ Respond to voices.

Figure 3.4. Sample sections from *Building Bridges Through Sensory Integration* (Yack, Sutton, & Aquilla, 1998).

**Olfactory (Smell) and
Gustatory (Taste) Systems**

Does your child:
- ❏ Dislike strong smells or tastes.
- ❏ Crave strong smells or tastes.
- ❏ Smear their feces.
- ❏ Eat non-edible foods.

Identifying Difficulties in Self-Care Skills
General Self-Care Checklist.

Touch:
- ❏ difficulty tolerating touch by a facecloth/towel.
- ❏ rubs the spot that was touched.
- ❏ seems to need rigid rituals.
- ❏ difficulty tolerating splashing in the bathtub.
- ❏ dislikes teeth brushing.
- ❏ complains that the toothbrush/hairbrush hurts them.
- ❏ can react aggressively to touch.
- ❏ dislikes hair brushing or anything on the head.
- ❏ dislikes touch on the bottom; from a diaper or toilet paper.
- ❏ wants to wear clothes all the time or may prefer to be naked.
- ❏ difficulty tolerating temperature change.

Proprioception
- ❏ constant dropping of objects *(toothpaste, brush, etc.).*
- ❏ too much/not enough pressure with objects of self care *(e.g., squeezes the toothpaste so tight that too much comes out, or unable to take the lid off).*
- ❏ really enjoys shower, rough toweling or firm hair brushing.
- ❏ unable to change body position to accommodate task *(e.g., lean head back to rinse shampoo).*

Vestibular:
- ❏ resistance to a change in head position/movement *(e.g., hair brushing or shampoo rinsing).*
- ❏ prefers to hold head upright.
- ❏ may become disoriented after a change in head position.
- ❏ difficulty with balance getting in and out of the tub, washing lower body.
- ❏ difficulty bending over the sink.
- ❏ fearful of sitting on the toilet, especially if feet are off the ground.

From: Yack, E., Sutton, S., & Aquilla, P. (1998). *Building Bridges Through Sensory Integration.* Used with permission by Building Bridges Through Sensory Integration, 132 Queen's Dr., Weston, Ont. M9N 2H6, Canada.

Figure 3.4. *(continued)*

Table 3.5

Some Questions to Guide Classroom Observations

Variable	Questions
Child	What are the child's strengths and difficulties in terms of motor skills, cognitive skills, communication, play and praxis?
	What methods does the child use to communicate?
	What are the child's preferred modes of interaction?
	Does the child imitate others? Does the child make eye contact?
	Does this fluctuate? In what way?
	What does the child enjoy or seek out?
	What are the child's specific behavioral concerns?
	When do they occur?
	What calms or arouses the child?
Task	What is required? Expected?
	How do others complete the task?
	Is the task clear and understandable?
	Is the task predictable?
	Does the task have a clear end? How does the child know when it is completed?
	Does the task have a clear sequence? How many steps are there?
	How are instructions provided?
	Is assistance available? What type?
	What materials are used?
	What are the sensory properties of the task and materials?
	How long is the task?

Environment and Context

Variable	Questions
Physical	What is the spatial arrangement of the area?
	What is the size of the area?
	Which objects and people are present?
	How is the area organized?
	How easily can the child move within the area?
	What is the temperature?
	What is the noise level?
	How densely packed are people and objects?
	What time of day is it?
	What odors are present?
	What is the lighting source?
	How visually stimulating is the area?

Table 3.5 (continued)
Some Questions to Guide Classroom Observations

Variable	Questions

Environment and Context

Social   Who is with the child?
With whom does the child choose to interact?
Who encourages the child's best performance?
What form of interaction occurs with peers? Teachers?
Other adults?

Cultural   What is expected within this environment?
Are the expectations or rules of the environment clear?
How are rules communicated?

From: Kienz, K., & Miller, H. (1999, March). Classroom evaluation of the child with autism. *School System. Special Interest Section Quarterly, 6*(1), p. 4. Used with permission by Therapy Association, Inc., PO Box 31220, Bethesda, MD 20824-1220.

The *Motivation Assessment Scale* contains 16 items in the (a) sensory, (b) escape, (c) attention, and (d) tangible areas, which are scored on a 6-point Likert scale to indicate whether a specific behavior occurs *never, almost never, seldom, half the time, usually, almost always,* or *always.* This instrument does not break the behavior into specific sensory areas but merely identifies whether the behavior has a sensory basis. The scale is often used as a screening tool for a problem behavior. If sensory issues are indicated as a probable reason for a given behavior, followup measures are typically administered to provide more specific sensory information.

The *Motivation Assessment Scale* can be completed by anyone familiar with the child who has observed the behavior of concern. It can be completed and scored in less than 10 minutes and can be used to investigate possible causes of behavior in individuals at any age. A copy of a *Motivation Assessment Scale* protocol appears in Figure 3.5.

Motivation Assessment Scale
by V. Mark Durand and Daniel B. Crimmins

Name _____ Rater _____ Date _____

Behavior Description _____

Setting Description _____

ITEM	NEVER	ALMOST NEVER	SELDOM	HALF THE TIME	USUALLY	ALMOST ALWAYS	ALWAYS
RESPONSE							
1. Would the behavior occur continuously, over and over, if this person was left alone for long periods of time? (For example, several hours.)	0	1	2	3	4	5	6
2. Does the behavior occur following a request to perform a difficult task?	0	1	2	3	4	5	6
3. Does the behavior seem to occur in response to your talking to other persons in the room?	0	1	2	3	4	5	6
4. Does the behavior ever occur to get a toy, food or activity that this person has been told that he or she can't have?	0	1	2	3	4	5	6
5. Would the behavior occur repeatedly, in the same way, for very long periods of time, if no one was around? (For example, rocking back and forth for over an hour.)	0	1	2	3	4	5	6
6. Does the behavior occur when any request is made of this person?	0	1	2	3	4	5	6
7. Does the behavior occur whenever you stop attending to this person?	0	1	2	3	4	5	6
8. Does the behavior occur when you take away a favorite toy, food, or activity?	0	1	2	3	4	5	6
9. Does it appear to you that this person enjoys performing the behavior? (It feels, tastes, looks, smells, and/or sounds pleasing.)	0	1	2	3	4	5	6
10. Does this person seem to do the behavior to upset or annoy you when you are trying to get him or her to do what you ask?	0	1	2	3	4	5	6

Figure 3.5. Sample: *Motivation Assessment Scale* protocol.

ITEM	RESPONSE						
	NEVER	ALMOST NEVER	SELDOM	HALF THE TIME	USUALLY	ALMOST ALWAYS	ALWAYS
11. Does this person seem to do the behavior to upset or annoy you when you are not paying attention to him or her? (For example, if you are sitting in a separate room, interacting with another person.)	0	1	2	3	4	5	6
12. Does the behavior stop occurring shortly after you give this person the toy, food or activity he or she has requested?	0	1	2	3	4	5	6
13. When the behavior is occurring, does this person seem calm and unaware of anything else going on around him or her?	0	1	2	3	4	5	6
14. Does the behavior stop occurring shortly after (one to five minutes) you stop working or making demands of this person?	0	1	2	3	4	5	6
15. Does this person seem to do the behavior to get you to spend some time with him or her?	0	1	2	3	4	5	6
16. Does the behavior seem to occur when this person has been told that he or she can't do something he or she had wanted to do?	0	1	2	3	4	5	6

SCORING

	Sensory	Escape	Attention	Tangible
	1. _____	2. _____	3. _____	4. _____
	5. _____	6. _____	7. _____	8. _____
	9. _____	10. _____	11. _____	12. _____
	13. _____	14. _____	15. _____	16. _____
Total score =	_____	_____	_____	_____
Mean score =	_____	_____	_____	_____
Relative ranking =	_____	_____	_____	_____

Figure 3.5 (continued)

Interpretation

Interpretations of assessment measures are largely instrument-dependent. As mentioned in the discussion of individual instruments, interpretations of results of sensory-related assessments or observations are most often made by occupational therapists or other professionals trained in sensory integration, who are skilled in administering, scoring, and interpreting this type of information. Skilled interpretations provide a comprehensive look at the child across environments, under various settings, with different adults and peers, and so on. In all cases, these individuals must be careful not to go beyond the intention of the instruments.

To be useful, recommendations that stem from an assessment must be detailed enough for implementation by the many staff members and parents who have contact with the child. The sensory information will help teachers and parents develop programming strategies that support the child's success in various environments. For example, assessment revealed that Jon has vestibular processing issues that appear to impact his ability to sit still and attend. As a result, at his IEP meeting, his teachers and parents discussed strategies that would address these needs. They thought that a Disc 'O' Sit™, an inflatable disc, or camping pillow would provide Jon with the needed vestibular input and help him sit in his chair and pay attention. Close collaboration among the occupational therapist and other team members in implementing the recommendations is essential to ensure that (a) recommendations are implemented effectively and safely and (b) that the interventions are directly addressing the child's needs and supporting her performance across environments.

- ASPERGER SYNDROME AND SENSORY ISSUES

INTERVENTIONS
FOR SENSORY ISSUES

A variety of behaviors exhibited in school, home, and community are problematic for many children and youth with Asperger Syndrome, interfering with their ability to make and keep friends as well as meet the demands of school. Understanding that behaviors may have underlying sensory components helps guide us in interpreting and planning strategies to support the child across settings. We would not presume to suggest that sensory strategies be implemented for ALL behaviors exhibited by individuals with Asperger Syndrome. As previously mentioned, behaviors occur in children and youth with Asperger Syndrome that do not have a sensory basis.

The chapter starts out with a brief overview of some programs that address sensory issues. Based on the premise that all behaviors have a purpose, the chapter then goes on to focus on intervention strategies that address behaviors often seen in children with Asperger Syndrome that may have a sensory basis.

Selected Publications and Programs That Address the Sensory Needs of Children and Youth with Asperger Syndrome

Several programs appear effective in meeting the sensory needs of children and youth with AS. We have not attempted to provide a comprehensive list but have highlighted some of the programs with which we have experienced success in working with individuals with AS. These include (a) *How Does Your Engine Run?: The Alert Program for Self-Regulation* (Williams & Shellenberger, 1996); (b) *The Tool Chest for*

Teachers, Parents, and Students (Henry Occupational Therapy Services, 1998); and (c) *Building Bridges Through Sensory Integration* (Yack, Sutton, & Aquilla, 1998).

How Does Your Engine Run?: The Alert Program for Self-Regulation (Williams & Shellenberger, 1996)

The ultimate goal in working in the sensory area is to help the child develop insight about his own sensory issues. Williams and Shellenberger (1996) have developed a comprehensive program, *How Does Your Engine Run?: The Alert Program for Self-Regulation*, specifically designed to meet this goal. Intended for use by occupational therapists in conjunction with educators and parents, this unique program helps children recognize their sensory needs. In addition, children and youth learn to recognize their level of alertness or arousal and to change that level as necessary to meet academic or social demands. The Alert Program "uses the analogy of an automobile engine, sometimes it runs on high, sometimes it runs on low, and sometimes it runs just right" (Williams & Shellenberger, 1996, pp. 2-1). The authors provide instruction in 3 stages and 12 mile markers (see Table 4.1), using a variety of visual supports that help children determine "how their engine is running." Interventions are grouped into five categories: (a) put something in your mouth, (b) move, (c) touch, (d) look, and (e) listen. In addition to helping children understand their sensory systems and learn how to recognize strategies that will help them be better learners, Williams and Shellenberger have also developed materials to assist adults in determining their sensory-motor preferences. Included in this book is the *Sensory-Motor Preference Checklist (for Adults)*, which works toward this end (see Figure 4.1).

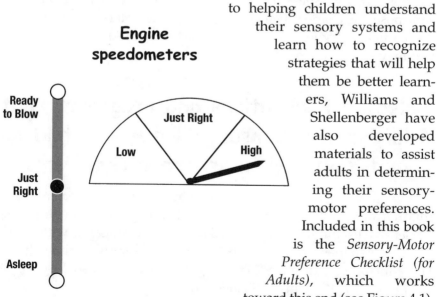

66

Table 4.1
3 Stages and 12 Mile Markers
of the Alert Program

Stage One: Identifying Engine Speeds

1. Students learn the engine words.

2. Adults level their own engine levels.

3. Students develop awareness of the feel of their own engine speeds, using the adults' labels as their guides.

4. Students learn to identify and label levels for themselves.

5. Students label levels for themselves, outside therapy sessions.

Stage Two: Experimenting with Methods to Change Engine Speeds

6. Leaders introduce sensorimotor methods to change engine levels.

7. Leaders identify sensorimotor preferences and sensory hypersensitivities.

8. Students begin experimentation with choosing strategies.

Stage Three: Regulating Engine Speeds

9. Students choose strategies independently.

10. Students use strategies independently, outside therapy sessions.

11. Students learn to change engine levels when options are limited.

From: Williams, M. S., & Shellenberger, S. (1996). *How does your engine run? A leader's guide to the alert program for self-regulation.* Used with permission of TherapyWorks, Inc., 4901 Butte Place N. W., Albuquerque, NM 87120.

Sensory-Motor Preference Checklist (For Adults)
(Williams & Shellenberger, 1996)

Directions: This checklist was developed to help adults recognize what strategies their own nervous systems employ to attain an appropriate state of alertness. Mark the items below that you use to increase (↑) or to decrease (↓) your state of alertness. You might mark both (↑ ↓) on some items. Others you might not use at all.

Put something in your mouth (Oral Motor Input)

__ drink a milkshake

__ suck on hard candy

__ crunch or suck on ice pieces

__ tongue in cheek movements

__ "chew" on pencil/pen

__ chew on coffee swizzle sticks

__ take slow, deep breaths

__ suck, lick, bite on your lips or the inside of your cheeks

__ drink carbonated drink

__ eat a cold popsicle

__ eat a pickle

__ chew gum

__ crunch on nuts/pretzels/chips

__ bite on nails/cuticle

__ eat popcorn/cut up vegetables

__ eat chips and a spicy dip

__ smoke cigarettes

__ chew on buttons, sweatshirt strings or collars

__ whistle while you work

__ drink coffee/tea (caffeinated)

__ drink hot cocoa or warm milk

__ other:

Move (Vestibular/Proprioceptive Input):

__ rock in a rocking chair

__ shift or "squirm" in a chair

__ push chair back on 2 legs

__ aerobic exercise

__ isometrics/lift weights

__ rock own body slightly

__ scrub kitchen floor

__ sit with crossed legs and bounce one slightly

__ roll neck and head slowly

__ run/jog

__ ride bike

__ tap toe, heel or foot

__ dance

__ tap pencil/pen

__ yard work

__ stretch/shake body parts

__ other:

Touch (Tactile Input):

__ twist own hair

__ move keys or coins in pocket with your hand

__ cool shower

__ warm bath

__ receive a massage

__ pet a dog or cat

__ drum fingers or pencil on table

__ rub gently on skin/clothes

Figure 4.1. Sample items from *Sensory-Motor Preference Checklist* (for adults).

Touch (Tactile Input) continued:
Fidget with the following:
__ a straw
__ paper clips
__ cuticle/nails
__ pencil/pen

__ earring or necklace
__ phone cord while talking
__ put fingers near mouth, eye, or nose
__ other:

Look (Visual Input):

__ open window shades after a
    boring movie in a classroom
__ watch a fireplace
__ watch a fish tank
__ watch sunset/sunrise
__ watch "oil and water" toys

How do you react to:
__ dim lighting
__ fluorescent lighting
__ sunlight through bedroom
    window when sleeping
__ rose-colored room
__ a "cluttered desk" when needing
    to concentrate

Listen (Auditory Input):

__ listen to classical music
__ listen to hard rock
__ listen to others "hum"
__ work in "quiet" room
__ work in "noisy" room
__ sing or talk to self

How do you react to:
__ scratch on chalkboard
__ "squeak" of a mechanical pencil
__ fire siren
__ waking to an unusual nosie
__ dog barking (almost constantly)

Questions to Ponder

1. Review this *Sensory-Motor Preference Checklist.* Think about what you do in a small, subtle manner to maintain an appropriate alert level that a child with a less mature nervous system may need to do in a larger, more intense way.

2. Notice which types of sensory input are comforting to your nervous system and which types of sensory input bother your nervous system. Are your items clustered in a certain category of sensory input?

3. Consider how often (frequency), how long (duration), how much (intensity), and with what rhythm (fast, slow, uneven, or even) you use these inputs to change your state of alertness.

From: Williams, M.S., & Shellenberger, S. (1996). *How does your engine run?: A leader's guide to the Alert Program for self-regulation.* Used with permission of TherapyWorks, 4901 Butte Place, N.W., Albuquerque, NM 87120.

Figure 4.1. *(continued)*

The Tool Chest for Teachers, Parents, and Students **(Henry Occupational Therapy Services, 1998)**

This resource provides 26 activities to assist educators and parents in helping children meet their sensory needs. This self-guided handbook discusses how to identify what a behavior may be communicating and how to develop strategies that will prevent behavior problems from occurring. Each activity outlines its benefits, where to begin, strategy instructions, additional projects, and supplies needed. The text is supplemented by two videos, *Tools for Teachers: Sensory Integration in the Schools* (Henry Occupational Therapy Services, 1998) and *Tools for Students: Tool Chest Activities for Home and School* (Henry Occupational Therapy Services, 1998), that overview the importance of sensory tools for the classroom and provide demonstrations of activities in school and home.

Building Bridges Through Sensory Integration **(Yack, Sutton, & Aquilla, 1998)**

Designed to help educators and parents develop insight into the sensory needs of children, this books specifically focuses on children who have been diagnosed with autism or other pervasive developmental disorders. The authors provide a detailed introduction to occupational therapy and its role in providing sensory integration activities for children. Within this resource, user-friendly checklists help the reader identify children's difficulties in (a) general self-care, (b) dressing, (c) eating, (d) school/work, (e) play, and (f) social skills. In addition, activities are included that address environmental and behavioral accommodations.

Incidents, Interpretations, and Interventions

In an effort to make it easier for you to find interventions for specific behaviors that a child demonstrates, this chapter contains a table that lists the behaviors using common terminology. Information is organized using the following categories:

- **incident** – describes the behavior you may see
- **interpretation** – possible sensory-based reason(s) why the behavior occurs
- **intervention** – strategies that may provide sensory-based support

Using the analogy of the sensory detective in Chapter 3, we might say that Incident, Interpretation, and Intervention are three "informants," who identify a behavior, determine the cause(s), and then solve the puzzle by offering appropriate interventions.

Many of the interventions are easy to implement at school and home. However, it is always best for parents and educators to work together as a team to pinpoint the behavior a child exhibits (incident), its cause (interpretation), and practical solutions (intervention). An occupational therapist or someone trained in sensory integration can be a particularly valuable multidisciplinary team member (see Table 4.2).

Summary

Children and youth with Asperger Syndrome have complex needs. As a result, strategies that are effective one day may not work the next. In addition, some strategies may not be appropriate at all for your child or student. Due to the complexities of these issues, consider tolerating sensory behaviors that are not keeping the child from participating in daily activities or disrupting others, thereby respecting his preferences and individual sensory systems. Occupational therapists and others trained in sensory integration techniques can provide valuable assistance in selecting and using strategies. Be creative and trust your instincts. Be a detective, but do not spend so much time analyzing behaviors that you miss opportunities to enjoy the child's individuality. By using the information and suggestions presented in this book, you can help the child with Asperger Syndrome "make sense" of her world.

Table 4.2

Incidents, Interpretations, and Interventions

Incident	Interpretation	Intervention
ACCIDENT PRONE		
Has trouble pouring and carrying without spilling	• Has trouble with motor planning related to successfully completing task. • May require additional proprioceptive input to judge body movements and adjustments needed.	• Increase the weight of the container while decreasing the amount of liquid in it. • Use dishes that are heavier to carry. • Have the child carry items to the table, using containers that will not spill on the way to the table. • Fill cups or bowls only partially.
Is clumsy/accident prone; bumps into things and breaks things often.	• Difficulty judging body positioning in relation to objects in the environment.	• Provide proprioceptive input using weighted vest, or ankle or wrist weights. • Teach the child to visually monitor movements in the environment.
Seems impulsive or hurries through things, including being unaware of safety issues.	• May have difficulty planning and including all steps in the appropriate order of performance. • May be avoiding contact with materials or activities that are perceived as unpleasant.	• Break the activity into steps and ask the child to perform one step at a time, completing each step before moving on. • Have someone model the activity first. • Use a visual for each step. • Reinforce completion of each step instead of just the final project. • Consider tactile sensitivity or avoidance and provide an alternate material with less threatening sensory features (i.e., use a cotton swab to glue on small pieces of the art activity instead of getting glue on fingers). • Consider a cooperative assignment where different steps can be distributed among students.

Note. Some incidents, interpretations and interventions appear in more than one topic area to help readers find the behavior of interest.

Table 4.2 *(continued)*

Incident	Interpretation	Intervention
ATTENTION		
Doesn't seem to understand body language or facial expressions.	• May be uncomfortable directing visual attention to body parts, body movements, or the faces of others. • May have difficulty processing the many changes in body movements and facial expressions. • May have problems distinguishing meaningful visual information from competing visual background detail. • Awareness of other individuals in the surrounding environment may be limited by intense preoccupation or focus. • Maintaining a distance from others to avoid physical touch could limit ability to perceive body language and facial expressions. • May be reliant on auditory information to guide actions.	• Provide auditory cue to direct attention. • Use an inflatable disc or camping pillow during times when concentration is needed. • Teach the meanings of facial expressions, specific body postures and gestures. • Whenever possible, eliminate some of the background distractors that may be present in the environment. • Respect the individual's need for distance to avoid physical touch. Verbally reassure her. Request that she watch you for specific cues. • Accompany facial expressions, gestures and body language with spoken language. • Be aware of the use of unspoken cues when delivering instruction. • Try to use as few sensory modalities at a time as possible.
Has problems making eye contact with others.	• Peripheral visual information may be more comfortable or useful than central vision. • May be difficult to "look" and "listen" at the same time. • May lack confidence about abilities.	• Consider decreasing expectation of "eye contact" in some situations and contexts. • Position in "line of sight" without getting too close. • Provide minimal auditory or slight tactile cue to encourage visual attention.

Table 4.2 *(continued)*

Incident	Interpretation	Intervention
ATTENTION *(continued)*		
	• Movement activities may be more comfortable or successful if the child is able to fix visual gaze on something besides another person.	• Incorporate activities that facilitate looking through labeling, turn taking and obtaining information and objects from others. Example: Have the child swing while asking him to label items being shown to him, held near the adult's face. • Break down tasks to smaller steps where success will be more readily achieved. • Provide imitation opportunities and activities for child to repeat a modeled behavior or action.
Stares intensely at people	• Has difficulty knowing which stimuli to attend to. • May need additional time to process information from his environment. • Visual acuity may be less than optimal. • Has a low tolerance for movement, subsequently limiting head movements. • Auditory comprehension problems may cause child to seek more intense visual information to compensate. • May be visually fixing on a target not related to the task as a way to aid in concentration or to prevent sensory overload.	• Develop auditory or visual cues that the child can use to help him know what to attend to. • Provide direct instruction on how to shift attention. Use imitation games (i.e., "Simon Says") to reinforce the skill. • Provide a written script that tells the student how to shift attention. • Provide a social story that discusses how others feel when people stare at them.

Table 4.2 *(continued)*

Incident	Interpretation	Intervention
BEHAVIOR IN GROUPS		
Doesn't seem to understand body language or facial expressions.	• May be uncomfortable directing visual attention to body parts, body movements, or the faces of others. • May have difficulty processing the many changes in body movements and facial expressions. • May have problems distinguishing meaningful visual information from competing visual background detail. • Awareness of other individuals in the surrounding environment may be limited by intense preoccupation or focus. • Maintaining a distance from others to avoid physical touch could limit ability to perceive body language and facial expressions. • May be reliant on auditory information to guide actions.	• Provide auditory cue to direct attention. • Use a Disc 'O' Sit™ or camping pillow during times when concentration is needed. • Teach the meanings of facial expressions, specific body postures, and gestures. • Whenever possible, eliminate some of the background distractors that may be present in the environment. • Respect the individual's need for distance to avoid physical touch. • Verbally reassure her. Request that she watch you for specific cues. • Accompany facial expressions, gestures, and body language with spoken language. • Be aware of the use of unspoken cues when delivering instruction. • Try to use as few sensory modalities at a time as possible.
Has difficulty keeping hands and feet to self when sitting in groups.	• Craves tactile input. • Doesn't understand about personal boundaries. • May learn by handling or manipulating objects.	• Provide visual or physical boundaries for sitting such as tape boundaries, carpet squares, placemats, inflatable disc, or camping pillow. • Provide a "fidget item" such as a Koosh Ball™ or Tangle™. Often fidget items can be academically

75

Table 4.2 (continued)

Incident	Interpretation	Intervention
BEHAVIOR IN GROUPS *(continued)*		
		related, such as holding a play cow when studying farm animals or grasping a squeeze/stress ball that looks like a planet when studying the solar system. • If the reaction occurs during a floor-based activity, have child lie on her stomach, propping her head on her elbows. • Have child hold or squeeze a large pillow held in lap.
Has difficulty regulating reactions in the lunchroom, including tantruming, screaming, or refusing to cooperate.	• Situations that have loud echoes, noise, movement, and strong scents can be stressful.	• Allow the child to go to the cafeteria early. • Allow the child to eat in the classroom or other nonstimulating environment. • Decrease time in the lunchroom. • Assist the child in setting up for the meal (opening milk, condiments, helping to select food).
Has problems making eye contact with others.	• Peripheral visual information may be more comfortable or useful than central vision. • May be difficult to "look" and "listen" at the same time. • May lack confidence in abilities. • Movement activities may be more comfortable or successful if the child is able to fix visual gaze on something besides another person.	• Consider decreasing expectation of "eye contact" in some situations and contexts. • Position in "line of sight" without getting too close. • Provide minimal auditory or slight tactile cue to encourage visual attention. • Incorporate activities that facilitate looking through labeling, turn taking, and obtaining information and objects from others. Example: Have the child swing while asking him to label items being shown to him, held near the adult's face. • Break down tasks to smaller steps where success will be more readily achieved.

Table 4.2 *(continued)*

Incident	Interpretation	Intervention
BEHAVIOR IN GROUPS *(continued)*		
		• Provide imitation opportunities and activities for child to repeat a modeled behavior or action.
Leans on peers while in line, sitting in groups, or sitting at table.	• May have poor postural control. • May require proprioceptive or vestibular input; his central nervous system may need "waking up."	• Provide opportunities for large-motor activities such as jumping, pulling and pushing prior to these activities. • Allow the child to stand during activities. • Provide the child legitimate opportunities to move, such as sharpening pencils or throwing away trash. • Place rubberized shelf-lining or Dycem™ on the seat of the chair. • Place a tennis ball on two chair legs (diagonal). This allows for continual small movements.
Steps on peers' heels/feet when walking, misses the chair when attempting to sit down, or sits on peers when group is sitting on the floor.	• Poor awareness. • Difficulty planning motor actions. • May have poor proprioceptive processing.	• At the preschool or early elementary level consider having the child hop, skip, do jumping jacks, bend down and touch toes half way down the hall (depending on motor planning ability). These activities may also be effective if done within the classroom just before walking down the hall. • Consider placing the student at the front or back of the line. • Ensure appropriate amount of spacing between students in line. • Instruct the child to carry her books against her body with hands touching opposite elbows. • Teach the child a song that she can sing to herself while walking down the hall (*Personal Space Invaders*, Lyons, 1997).

Table 4.2 *(continued)*

Incident	Interpretation	Intervention
DRESSING/CLOTHES		
Always looks unkempt/sloppy.	• Has decreased body awareness or has difficulty "feeling" that his clothes are not on straight.	• Create a visual schedule for getting ready. • Have the child wear clothing that is "snug" to provide an increased awareness. • Teach the child a sequential strategy for evaluating appearance (i.e., when leaving for the bus stop, check mirror for combed hair, no toothpaste on mouth, shirt buttoned correctly, pants zipped, shoes tied).
Can't stand sand in shoes or bumps of seams in socks.	• Feel of sand or seams is extremely uncomfortable.	• Turn socks inside out so the seam is on the outside. • Try different socks where the seams are not as prominent. • Be aware of the type of shoes the child is wearing. • Select shoes for comfort, not style.
Dislikes certain clothes.	• Certain textures or materials may be more irritating than others. • Characteristics of specific items may be irritating and uncomfortable for the child such as sleeve length or certain forms of waistbands. Some dislike the sound of nylon or corduroy pants when walking.	• Respect the child's desire for certain textures when appropriate. • Consult a trained therapist regarding a brushing program. • Rub lotion on the child. • Massage the child with a vigorous towel rub to increase tolerance to certain textures of clothing items and then introduce a new item or texture. • Remove clothing tags that may cause irritation. • Use one detergent consistently. • Consider a fragrance-free detergent.

Table 4.2 *(continued)*

Incident	Interpretation	Intervention
DRESSING/CLOTHES *(continued)*		
Refuses to go barefoot, especially in grass.	• Feet may be very sensitive.	• Try rubbing the child's feet with a cloth or towel first. • Introduce new textures to the child's feet such as sand, beans, rice, bubble wrap, or Contact Paper™. Offer but do not force these activities. • Provide the child with socks that have a new "feel."
Trouble dressing, especially clothes with fasteners.	• Has difficulty with fine-motor skills. • May have weak hand muscles.	• Have the child work with Velcro fasteners. • Begin with larger fasteners or buttons. Once these have been mastered, move to smaller fasteners or buttons. • Buy clothes that have few or no fasteners. • Tell the child to look as she fastens. • Instruct the child to start with the bottom fastener, snap, or button. • Use activities to increase hand strength (i.e., using therapy putty, clay or Playdoh™ with small objects hidden within it. Have the child pull the therapy putty apart to look for the items.
Wears clothing inappropriate for the situation – no boots or coat in snow.	• Texture and style of clothing may be irritating.	• Ensure that clothes apply the appropriate pressure and are of a texture that is comfortable to the child. • Make allowances for individual preferences, when appropriate. • Gradually introduce new clothes. For example, for younger children introduce an item that a favorite doll can wear. For older children, introduce a new item that contains a desired logo or television character.

Table 4.2 *(continued)*

Incident	Interpretation	Intervention
EATING/CHEWING		
Chews on clothing, pens, pencils.	• May find this calming. • May be seeking proprioceptive input. • May like the tactile input of the item.	• Allow the child to chew on gum, gummy worms (chill to harden), jujubes, hard candy, coffee stirrers, latex-free tubing, straws, or have snacks that are crunchy or chewy. • Allow the child to chew on clothes if it does not cause harm. • Provide a water bottle with a sturdy straw that the child can drink from. • Consider alternatives with a strong oral emphasis.
Is easily distracted/ nauseated by certain smells.	• May be oversensitive to certain smells and become very irritated when exposed to them.	• Use unscented detergents or shampoos. • Refrain from wearing perfumes or aftershave lotions that are irritating to the child. • Make the environment as fragrance-free as possible.
Is easily distracted/ nauseated by certain tastes.	• May be very sensitive to certain textures or tastes of foods.	• Respect individual differences if nutrition is not compromised. • Change one characteristic of food at a time. If the child likes fruit, dehydrate the fruit to introduce a new texture. Mix two preferred fruits. • Introduce very small bites or portions.
Messy eater; prefers to use fingers rather than utensils to eat.	• May be unable to "feel" the sensation around the mouth area. • Dislikes the feel of the utensils in his mouth or hands. • May have poor fine-motor skills.	• Massage lightly around the child's mouth using different materials and textures such as washcloths, soft-bristled toothbrush, or mini-vibrating toothbrush. • Encourage activities that involve the mouth (i.e., whistles, bubble wands, kazoos).

Table 4.2 *(continued)*

Incident	Interpretation	Intervention
EATING/CHEWING *(continued)*		
Won't eat certain foods.	• Texture of the food may not be pleasant. • May be sensitive to the temperature of the food items. • May be oversensitive to certain tastes.	• Allow the child to choose foods as long as nutrition is not compromised. • Apply deep pressure to teeth and gums using a hard, yet pliable item. For example, chewing on rubber tubing or a straw may help the child. • Introduce new foods by expanding one sensory characteristic at a time. For example, if the child eats yogurt, introduce corn flakes, oat flakes, or grape nuts into the yogurt to provide texture.
EMOTIONS/FEELINGS/ RELATIONSHIPS		
Appears to like father's touch better than mother's.	• Mother's touch may be too light. • May not anticipate mother's touch because mother walks up quietly behind the child. Father's touch may be anticipated because the child may hear father coming or father may always approach head-on.	• Make the child aware that touch is coming. • Mother and all familiy and team members should use deep pressure when possible as this is usually more calming and less uncomfortable. • Allow the child to initiate the touch.

Table 4.2 *(continued)*

Incident	Interpretation	Intervention
EMOTIONS/FEELINGS/ RELATIONSHIPS *(continued)*		
Dislikes being hugged or kissed, but is okay when he initiates.	• Touch may be uncomfortable if unexpected.	• When appropriate, allow the child to determine when he will hug or kiss. • Enlighten family members or friends about the child's preferences to avoid uncomfortable and embarrassing situations. • Let the child know before a hug or kiss takes place.
Has difficulty making friends.	• Poor motor planning skills impact success at group activities and games. • Decreased (hyposensitivity) awareness of food and materials on face and hands limits social acceptance. • Hypersensitivity to incidental or unplanned touch may result in reactionary behaviors not understood by others. • May fail to observe and comprehend the meaning of gestures and facial expressions. • Self-talk and other anxiety-reducing behaviors may interfere with conversational skills.	• Establish a structured recess activity with preassigned roles that can be practiced in isolation. • Teach a self-care routine such as using a napkin after every 3 bites or handwashing following each recess. • Practice a socially acceptable "script" that could be expressed by the child when unexpectedly bumped. • Teach the child how to approach an individual or group as well as the skills needed to interact with peers. • Provide direct instruction for common gestures and expressions with opportunities to practice observation skills in a nonthreatening situation. • Provide a hand fidget that can be discreetly manipulated, leaving visual attention available. • Develop a "Circle of Friends," "Lunch Bunch," or "Recess Buddies" for the child.

Table 4.2 *(continued)*

Incident	Interpretation	Intervention
EMOTIONS/FEELINGS/ RELATIONSHIPS *(continued)*		
	• Restricted interest or preoccupation with objects or activities may decrease sensory availability for other people and things in the environment, impacting opportunities for spontaneous play. • Unpredictable emotional reactions may impact the child's ability to form friendships.	• Develop an integrated play group that involves the child and typical peers that will include various sensory motor activities.
Is sensitive to criticism.	• May have poor self-concept about abilities based on motor planning difficulties that result in uncoordinated movements. • Overconfidence may be a defense mechanism for coping with motor planning difficulties. • May be reacting to sensory characteristics of the person providing the criticism (i.e., voice quality, volume, pitch) rather than the criticism itself. • Anxiety about skills or performance affects ability to generate ideas or problem-solve.	• Deliver feedback in a positive manner at a time when the child is emotionally available. • Consider providing feedback visually through cartooning, social stories, or social autopsy. • Provide opportunities for the child to identify his strengths and discuss characteristics that can be a concern. • Present potentially difficult tasks with models, written or pictorial directions, and structure. • Model how to react to criticism. • Teach the child a strategy of how to respond to criticism.

Table 4.2 *(continued)*

Incident	Interpretation	Intervention
GROOMING		
Dislikes having face or hair washed.	• Light touch may be painful·or annoying.	• Allow the child to wash her own hair. The response is often less defensive if the child regulates the touching herself. • Use firm pressure. Deep pressure does not elicit as strong an emotional response. • Let the child know she is going to be touched before it occurs.
Dislikes toothbrushing.	• Toothbrush may be too big or the bristles too hard. • Taste or texture of the toothpaste may be irritating to the child's nervous system.	• Consider a smaller toothbrush with softer bristles or a toothbrush that vibrates. • If possible, let the child control his own toothbrush. That way, he can control the amount of pressure that is comfortable to tolerate. • Select toothpaste that tastes good to the child. • Monitor the amount of toothpaste on the toothbrush. • Consider dipping the damp toothbrush into the toothpaste instead of squeezing a "blob" on it.
Does not like having hair cut.	• May be sensitive to the movement and height or overall size of the barber chair. • Head movement required to lie back in sink may be unpleasant. • Errant spray from sink nozzle or spray bottle may be annoying. • Noise and vibration of clippers or scissors may be unsettling. • Visual and tactile sensitivity may be	• Provide a visual support that outlines the steps of getting a hair cut. • For the younger child, play-act giving a doll or stuffed animal a pretend haircut, verbally elaborating on the sensory aspects that are a part of the process. • Prepare child with verbal instruction such as "I'm going to raise the chair now." • Provide the opportunity for the child to make choices about the process. • Invite the child to participate in the process – "Do you want to spray your own hair?"

Table 4.2 *(continued)*

Incident	Interpretation	Intervention
GROOMING *(continued)*		
	triggered by close proximity of barber. • Sensation around neck and noise of vinyl drape may be uncomfortable. • Has trouble with feel of stray, cut hair on neck and clothes following haircut.	• Cut hair in a chair with surrounding support. Place pillows under and around child. • Provide favorable music, using earbuds to listen if needed. • Apply deep pressure to the child's head before beginning the hair cut. This can be done directly using the fingertips or a towel may be used to rub the head. • Allow the child to manipulate a fidget or hold a small vibrator in his hands while his hair is being cut. Give the child a Koosh™ ball, Theraputty™, or some sort of character with moveable body parts to play with during the hair cut. • Provide an alternative to the standard drape like a towel. • Bring fresh clothing for child to change into following the haircut. • Consider providing a preferred activity following the hair cut.
Does not like having nails cut.	• The actual cutting of the nail may be painful or uncomfortable for the child. • Having another person hold the child's finger may be uncomfortable for the child. • Fear of cutting too close to the quick or cutting skin may be anxiety-provoking.	• Rub the child's hands with lotion using deep pressure before beginning to cut the nails. • Cuticle scissors may be more tolerable than larger fingernail clippers. • Use an emery board in lieu of clipping nails to keep at a manageable length. • Try cutting the child's nails while he is interested in or distracted by something else, maybe even sleeping. • Cut nails as part of the bathing routine following playtime when the nail is softer and more pliable.

Table 4.2 *(continued)*

Incident	Interpretation	Intervention
GROOMING *(continued)*		
		• Break the task into smaller increments such as two fingers at a time over a period of time. • Have the child place fingers over a table or counter edge pressing down to provide deep pressure to the fingertip but leaving nail edge exposed for clipping. • Use a social story to describe the steps of nail clipping and the hygiene and social benefits of well-groomed nails.
MOVEMENT		
Has difficulty transitioning in hallways. (*Note.* Response may depend on amount of activity in the hallway.)	• May be touched unexpectedly by somebody. The touch may be misinterpreted as a hit, causing a defensive response. • Noise in the hall may be too loud. • Visual activity may be disorienting.	• Allow the child to be first or last in line. • Allow the child to leave class 5 minutes early. • Have the child carry something heavy to provide proprioceptive input. • Create a map that provides a visual plan or route between locations. • Have the child hold the door open for the rest of the class by leaning her back into the door. This extra input may help her tolerate the subsequent sensory input of the hall. • Consider preferential placement of locker (at the end of the row) to decrease opportunities for unintentional physical contact with other students.

Table 4.2 (continued)

Incident	Interpretation	Intervention
MOVEMENT (continued)		
Prefers only to engage in sedentary activities (i.e., television, computer, video games).	• Limiting actions may be a way to avoid activities that present unpleasant sensations and unpredictable movements. • May have poor self-concept about abilities based on motor planning difficulties that result in uncoordinated movements. • Anxiety about skills or performance affects his ability to generate ideas or problem-solve.	• Embed physical movement into routine activities such as making the bed, emptying the trash, pushing the book cart, etc. • Incorporate movement into the child's sedentary activity. For example, to play a video game, the child must first walk up a flight of stairs or get the video game from the highest shelf. • Add music to the task providing a structured starting and stopping point. • Utilize the child's area of interest to elaborate on the activity. • Provide a visual support that demonstrates the steps of a nonsedentary activity.
Steps on peers' heels/feet when talking, misses the chair when attempting to sit down, or sits on peers when group is sitting on the floor.	• Poor awareness. • Difficulty planning motor actions.	• At the preschool or early elementary level consider having the child hop, skip, do jumping jacks, bend down and touch toes half way down the hall (depending on motor planning ability). These activities may also be effective if done within the classroom just before walking down the hall. • Consider placing the student at the front or back of the line. • Ensure appropriate amount of spacing between students in line. • Instruct the child to carry her books against her body with hands touching opposite elbows. • Teach the child a song that she can sing to herself while walking down the hall (*Personal Space Invaders*, Lyons, 1997).

Table 4.2 *(continued)*

Incident	Interpretation	Intervention
NOISE/SOUND		
Does not notice sounds in the environment.	• Has a difficult time knowing which sounds to attend to. • May be so focused on what he is doing that the sound does not register. • May have difficulty perceiving specific pitches or frequencies.	• Plan activities that will help teach the child to attend to various sounds. Play games using various sounds found in the environment like an auditory bingo game. • Utilize a visual or tactile cue to gain the child's attention.
Does not respond when name is called.	• May be so focused on what she is doing that the sound does not register. • May have difficulty perceiving specific pitches or frequencies.	• Teach the child to attend to his name by using games that involve saying his name and then reinforcing him for responding. • Develop visual cues or signals to gain the child's attention. • Vary the intonation or add melody, using a "sing-song" manner. • Pair a novel auditory cue with name such as clicking fingers or clapping hands.
Easily distracted by and fearful of loud noise.	• May be hypersensitive to noises, especially when not prepared for them. • May have difficulty determining which noises or tones to attend to in the environment and which to disregard.	• Use soft talking or singing to help the child know what to attend to. • Use soft background noise for calming. • In situations or places where the child experiences a lot of loud noises, headphones or earplugs may be helpful to buffer some of the noise. • Whenever possible, alert or prepare the child before the offending noise occurs. • Avoid using appliances or equipment at times when you would like the child to maintain his focus.

Table 4.2 *(continued)*

NOISE/SOUND *(continued)*

Incident	Interpretation	Intervention
Has difficulty processing sounds.	• When exposed to several sounds at the same time, it may be difficult for the child to know which sounds to attend to and when to attend to them.	• Get the child's attention first. Give directions slowly, allowing time for the child to process in between each step. • After giving directions, ask the child to repeat what was said to check for accuracy. • Use body gestures and/or visual supports along with the verbal directions. • Make sure that quiet occurs before directions are given. • Teach a cue to use when the child needs to attend (i.e., hand signal, touch on the shoulder).
Hums constantly.	• May be overstimulated by classroom noise. The humming may block out noises that cause anxiety. • Seeks auditory or tactile input.	• If the noise or activity level is a concern, move the child away from the source of noise or activity. • If the child needs to hum to concentrate, teach the child to hum more quietly. • Allow the child to use and play with "vibration" by using such items as an electric toothbrush or a kazoo.
Is bothered by the noises of household appliances.	• Sometimes the pitch and frequency of household appliances can be very distracting and annoying to children who experience auditory issues.	• Expose the child to the "irritating" noise in small steps, gradually increasing the duration as tolerance improves. • Warn the child that the appliance is going to be turned on so she won't be taken by surprise. • Have the child participate in using the appliance, if appropriate. • Lessen the unpleasant effect of the noise by combining it with pleasant sound (music on the radio). • Pair the noise with a preferred activity.

Table 4.2 *(continued)*

Incident	Interpretation	Intervention
NOISE/SOUND *(continued)*		
Notices every little sound or visual change in the environment.	• These distractions can be overwhelming, making it difficult for the child to remain focused.	• Keep visual/auditory distractions to a minimum. • Set up a quiet place with a bean bag chair for the child. • Consider alternate seating away from distractions. • Prepare the child in advance for distractions such as announcements or visitors, using a visual support that reflects the anticipated change. • Consider using a visual barrier or "cubicle" for desk work. • Provide headphones or earplugs for the child to wear during testing or seatwork after verbal directives are given.
Talks self through a task.	• May need the added input to help keep himself focused and stay on task to completion. • Sound of own voice may block out other auditory input. • May have poor self-concept about abilities based on motor planning difficulties.	• Allow the child to do this if it does not interfere with others. • Utilize a hand fidget to help decrease anxiety or enhance self-regulation. • Provide a weighted lap pad for deep pressure input. • Develop visual supports for use in a situation where child is unable to talk himself through tasks without disturbing others. This might also give him the extra support to refocus and continue if he becomes distracted. • Teach the child to self-talk using a lower volume or standing away from others.

Table 4.2 *(continued)*

Incident	Interpretation	Intervention
ORGANIZATION		
Has poor organizational skills; constantly loses school materials; papers fall out of notebook.	• Has difficulty focusing on relevant stimuli. • Has difficulty discriminating the items he may need from other things in his desk.	• Provide visual structure through color coding or assignment books. • Use tape inside the desk as a boundary marker for books. • Organize materials under the desk or on a bookshelf so they are always visible. • Use a sturdy box lid to contain student materials. Slide the box into the desk where it serves as a laptop desk. • Provide a notebook to carry papers to and from home with clearly marked "Homework" sections for each subject.
Talks self through a task.	• May need the added input to help keep himself focused and stay on task to completion. • Sound of own voice may block out other auditory input. • May have poor self-concept about abilities based on motor planning difficulties.	• Allow the child to do this if it does not interfere with others. • Utilize a hand fidget to help decrease anxiety. • Provide a weighted lap pad for deep pressure input. • Develop visual supports for use in a situation where child is unable to talk himself through tasks without disturbing others. This might also give him the extra support to refocus and continue if he becomes distracted. • Teach the child to self-talk using a lower volume.

Table 4.2 *(continued)*

Incident	Interpretation	Intervention
PLAY		
Engages in rough play during recess, gym class, and organized sport activities.	• Has unclear understanding of own strength. • Seeks proprioceptive input. • May not be able to judge where her body is in relation to other children.	• Prior to contact sports, have the child participate in gross-motor activities (i.e., jumping, wheelbarrow races, crab crawls, tug-of-war) that increase body awareness. • Have the child wear a compression-type garment (Spandex™ or Lycra™) under regular clothes. • Make recess a series of planned activities that look like an obstacle course, including hanging by hands or feet, pushing, pulling, or jumping.
Is hesitant to access playground equipment or participate in games and play where feet lose contact with the ground.	• May be afraid of falling and needs the reassurance of being connected to the ground.	• Allow the child to direct the movement initially. • Grade the activity to a level with less challenge or threat to the child. • Provide supervised practice opportunities in advance of participation in the activity with others. • Incorporate additional proprioceptive stimulation with weight or tactile input by briskly rubbing prior to activity.

Table 4.2 *(continued)*

Incident	Interpretation	Intervention
ROUTINES		
Experiences difficulty when changes occur.	• A routine provides predictability and helps stay organized and focused. • Needs predictability, especially if his body does not "feel in control." • Feels the need to structure schedules and activities to avoid unpleasant sensory experiences. • Does not know what to do when change occurs.	• Offer the child a signal before a change occurs. • Prepare the child for changes using visual supports. • Provide deep pressure activities that the child may utilize when a change occurs. • Give the child a script to use when an unexpected event occurs. • Gradually incorporate "unplanned" activities into the schedule, starting with preferred activities. • Incorporate a "change" symbol into the child's schedule.
Has rigid rituals at home and school.	• Prefers to have predictability in his environment. • Feels the need to structure schedule and activities to avoid unpleasant sensory experiences. • Motor planning challenges motivate the child to engage only in activities he feels competent about.	• Honor the ritual whenever possible if it doesn't interfere with daily living activities. • Use visual supports/schedules to help the child to stay organized. • Make changes in the "usual" scheduling and offer strategies that the child can use to help him cope with these changes. • Identify possible triggers to ritualistic behaviors. Implement deep pressure and heavy work activities to organize. • Elaborate on the child's ritual by altering one sensory aspect at a time as a way to introduce flexibility. An example might be using a strong-scented or granular soap during a hand-washing routine. • Warn the child ahead of time that the ritual may be different. • Offer a quiet place for the child to help him calm down or reorganize. • Allow the child access to a swing or rocking chair.

Table 4.2 *(continued)*

Incident	Interpretation	Intervention
SITTING		
Crawls under desk.	• Needs to be away from distractions from others talking, lights buzzing, etc. • Needs her personal space defined.	• Provide a quiet area in the room for the child. The area could contain beanbags, large pillows, or a rocking chair. • Reinforce with positive feedback when the child lets you know he needs some "quiet time." • Provide a large barrel or small playhouse for sitting. • Wrap the child in a quilt. • Allow the child to sit in an upholstered chair with arms. • Seat the child away from distractors. • Seat the child near the teacher.
Has difficulty keeping hands and feet to self when sitting in groups.	• Craves tactile input. • Doesn't understand about personal boundaries. • May learn by handling or manipulating objects.	• Provide visual or physical boundaries for sitting such as tape boundaries, carpet squares, placemats, inflatable disc, or camping pillow. • Provide a "fidget item" such as a Koosh Ball™ or Tangle™. Often fidget items can be academically related, such as holding a play cow when studying farm animals or grasping a squeeze/stress ball that looks like a planet when studying the solar system. • If the reaction occurs during a floor-based activity, have child lie on her stomach, propping her head on her elbows. • Have a child hold or squeeze a large pillow held in lap.

Table 4.2 *(continued)*

Incident	Interpretation	Intervention
SITTING *(continued)*		
Sits with legs on top of chair back.	• Desk and chair may not fit student size. • May need additional proprioceptive input. May be self-regulating.	• If the child is not in danger of hurting himself, allow the behavior. • Ensure that desk and chair size are appropriate for child. • Provide inflatable disc, camping pillow, therapy ball or t-stool. • Allow the child to complete assignments while lying on the floor or standing by the desk. • Have the child sit on her legs. • Give frequent movement breaks.
SLEEPING		
Is a very restless sleeper.	• May be uncomfortable with the sheets on her bed as the light touch may be more irritating than calming. • May become distracted by light or noise while trying to sleep. • May not require "standard" amount of sleep due to medications or natural constitution. • May have difficulty with self-regulation.	• Have the child sleep in a sleeping bag and/or under a comforter. • Warm bedclothes in dryer. • Try using flannel sheets because cotton sheets often form little "pills" that may be irritating. • Before bedtime, rub the child with lotion or powder. This may be calming to her system, helping her to settle down to sleep. • What the child wears to bed might also impact her ability to sleep comfortably. Some children prefer heavy, tight-fitting pajamas, while others are more comfortable in a light-weight t-shirt. • Some children benefit from enclosing their bed in a tent-like manner to filter out light and noises. • Establishing a predictable routine for bedtime might help. • For some children, roughhouse play can be helpful to prepare them for sleep. For others it may be overstimulating.

Table 4.2 (continued)

Incident	Interpretation	Intervention
SLEEPING (continued)		
		• Consider giving the child a warm bath or shower prior to bedtime. • White noise may serve to calm the child. A fan or relaxing music may aid in sleep. • Provide water bottle with straw to drink at night if needed.
Prefers sleeping on the floor instead of bed.	• May prefer to remain close to the ground. • May not be comfortable in his bed because of the mattress or sheets.	• Allow the child to sleep on the floor in a sleeping bag. • Try placing the child's mattress on the floor. • Use flannel sheets, a sleeping bag, or heavy comforter. • Provide the child with a body pillow or stuffed animal.
TOUCHING		
Avoids messy materials such as paints, glue, shaving cream.	• Activities involving certain kinds of materials may be uncomfortable for the child.	• Encourage tolerance (without forcing) of these kinds of materials through controlled, gradual exposure to various items and textures. • Prepare the child for a given activity by providing a visual cue. • Plan activities that are uncomfortable followed by activities that the child likes. As the activity becomes more tolerable, gradually increase the length of time child is engaged in it.
Drags hands along walls when walking.	• Seeks tactile input. • Needs proprioceptive input to help him feel comfortable. • May like the feel of the wall.	• Allowing the child to do it. • Have the child carry something heavy. • Have the child carry something that has a texture and surface similar to the wall.

Table 4.2 *(continued)*

Incident	Interpretation	Intervention
TOUCHING *(continued)*		
		• If the child is young, have her hold the hand of a peer or adult. • Have the child hold on to a rope or classroom object. • Have the child carry a container holding the materials to be used in the next class or activity. • Provide proprioceptive or vestibular input by having the child hop, skip, do jumping jacks, or bend down and touch toes half way down the hall. • Instruct the child to carry her books against her body with hands touching opposite elbows.
Picks at scabs, lips and nose.	• May be anxious. • Reaction may calm and aid concentration. • Input may help increase alertness if the child is bored with surroundings. • Increased attention to a skin breakdown in various stages of healing may come from an itching or irritating tactile sensation.	• Provide fidget items such as Koosh Ball™, therapy putty, pliable art eraser, bookmark with a tassel, small toys or manipulatives. • Place a strip of Velcro™ (one or both sides) inside book binder or underneath the desk that the child can play with or pick at. • Use topical ointments or lubricants that may help to alleviate or alter the irritating sensory input.
Touches everything.	• May learn through touching. • May desire more tactile input.	• When possible, allow the child to explore. • Before the child enters the environment in which there are many items that are not to be touched, provide deep pressure by rubbing shoulders, back, or palms. • Accompany a touch by a verbal statement of the rules for touching. • Allow the child to hold an object that can provide deep pressure.

Table 4.2 *(continued)*

Incident	Interpretation	Intervention
WRITING/COLORING		
Has messy handwriting; unable to stay within the lines	• Does not receive the appropriate sensations to plan how to move and design a sequence of what comes next. • Feel of the pencil may interfere with an effective pencil grasp. • Creative writing or generating own sentences is more challenging than copying.	• Have the child engage in gross-motor activities before he is asked to perform fine-motor activities such as 5 chair push-ups or donkey kicks before writing. • Encourage the child to participate in activities that develop hand strength (i.e., wheelbarrow walking, crawling). • Hide items in therapy putty and ask the child to find them. This can be made more challenging by asking the child to do the activity using only one hand to pull the putty apart to retrieve the small items inside. • Emphasize movement with handwriting instruction, such as practicing large letters in the air or on the chalkboard. • Have the child write on "bumpy" paper with raised lines.
Holds pencils and crayons by fingertips only and only uses fingertips when feeling toys.	• Touching items with the palm of the hand may be uncomfortable. • May not have the appropriate amount of strength in her hands.	• Provide deep pressure input (using thumb to rub) to palm of child's hand prior to activity. • Encourage activities that require the hands to touch and hold materials and objects such as constructing toys and art projects. • Incorporate various textures during play such as beans or rice. • Use activities that progress from only using fingertips to involving the whole hand. Introduce finger paints, shaving cream and lotion first. Then move to activities requiring hands, such as holding a ball or playing with Playdoh™.

CHRISTOPHER'S STORY: A SENSORY PROCESSING CASE STUDY

The authors would like to thank Christopher's parents, Beth Rosemergey and Charles Orth; Lisa Steiner, Preschool Early Childhood Special Education Teacher, and Laurel Bohl, OTR/L, for sharing their memories and strategies described in this case study.

Christopher is seven years old and will be entering the second grade in the fall. He lives with his parents and one younger brother in a Midwestern suburb. Christopher's parents became concerned about his development when he did not begin speaking in sentences around the age of two. Christopher struggled and used few two- or three-word sentences at age three and frequently said his name as the subject of a sentence rather than "I." He had difficulty riding a tricycle and catching a ball and was generally described as clumsy. Besides these concerns about gross-motor skills, his fine-motor abilities were less developed than those of his same-aged peers. Specifically, Christopher avoided drawing, cutting, and coloring. For these reasons, his parents initiated an evaluation through a community children's hospital.

Medical Evaluation

Christopher was seen by a developmental pediatrician and given a diagnosis of Pervasive Developmental Disorder-Not Otherwise Specified (PDD-NOS) when he was four years old. Specific observations that led to this diagnosis included:

1. impairment in the use and interpretation of multiple nonverbal behaviors and gestures and difficulty developing peer relationships (qualitative impairments in social interactions),
2. difficulty initiating and sustaining a conversation with others, use of "Christopher" rather than "I" (qualitative impairment in communication), and
3. inflexible adherence to routines and rituals and intense interest in trains (restricted, repetitive patterns of behavior and interests).

Additional observations and testing indicated that Christopher was hyperlexic (he recognized letters of the alphabet before the age of two and a half years old). Behaviors that might reflect sensory processing issues included frequent chewing on his clothing and other toys/objects, varied attention span, and constant movement.

On formal achievement testing, he scored at or well above age level in all subtests except prewriting/drawing, where results were well below what would be expected for his age. The developmental pediatrician who performed the evaluation stated in her report that she felt that Christopher might be diagnosed in the future as having Asperger Syndrome.

Based on this initial evaluation, Christopher was referred to the hospital-based Pervasive Developmental Disorders Team (PDD Team) for a more thorough multidisciplinary evaluation. The team included a psychologist, a speech language pathologist, an occupational therapist, and the developmental pediatrician who made the referral.

The following information represents a summary of the PDD Team's assessment based on direct observation and administration of formal and informal assessment measures.

Cognitive/Adaptive: Cognitive testing indicated an IQ of 78 with strengths in short-term memory and weaker skills in quantitative reasoning and abstract visual reasoning. Standardized assessment of adaptive skills, based on parental report, fell in the impaired range with all adaptive areas being below expected levels for his age.

Communication: Chris' primary form of communication was verbal, although he did use some gestures, proximity, and eye gaze to communicate with others. Although he was able to answer simple "what" and some "where" questions, he was not able to answer "why" or "how" questions. Difficulties were also observed in pragmatics (e.g., topic maintenance, getting a listener's attention, turn taking in conversation) and Christopher was noted to perseverate on topics that were of interest to him (trains). Traditional audiometric assessment revealed that his hearing was within normal limits.

Sensory Processing: Based on behaviors observed during the assessment as well as parent information, Christopher was described as having a moderate sensory modulation disorder. He appeared to be a sensory seeker in response to vestibular and proprioceptive stimuli. Specifically, he sought vestibular (rocking and moving quickly about the room) and proprioceptive (rough play/wrestling with his dad, pressing his head into a pillow, pushing into a therapy ball with his hands and body) input in his environment. He was also noted to seek some tactile input, especially through mouthing and chewing activities (which also have a proprioceptive component), although he avoided other tactile input such as having his face washed, hair combed, and teeth brushed. He had a difficult time accepting unexpected touch or being cuddled. Additionally, Christopher was observed to have motor planning difficulties during gross-motor (e.g., hopping, catching a ball) and particularly during fine-motor tasks (e.g., coloring, drawing).

Christopher was described as having a moderate sensory modulation disorder.

Educational Evaluation

When the medical evaluations were completed, Christopher's parents initiated a referral to the local school district to determine whether their son would be eligible for special education services. As part of the assessment process for possible placement, Chris began attending the local school district's early childhood program three hours per day, four days a week. Evaluative reports from the hospital's PDD Team were shared with the district staff, and additional information was gathered to complete district requirements for eligibility. For example, his parents filled out a developmental history. Formal fine-motor and informal gross-motor testing was also completed. Gross-motor skills were assessed through observation by a physical therapist in the classroom and on the playground. This information is summarized below.

Developmental History

Prenatal/perinatal history included the inducement of labor due to a decreased amount of amniotic fluid. Developmental milestones were reported as follows:

sat	6 months
crawled	9 months
walked	13 months
repeated syllables	5 months
talked in sentences	3 years ("struggling")
toilet trained (toileting)	3 years (occasional daytime accidents; continued nighttime wetting)

The medical history was significant for recurrent upper-respiratory infections and middle-ear infections, for which tubes were placed when Christopher was 16 months old.

Christopher started attending a community preschool when he was three and a half years old. He was reported to be skilled at working puzzles, looking at books, talking about trains, and playing with family members. After a while the preschool teacher became concerned about Christopher's hearing and lack of eye contact and shared her observations with his parents. At school, he struggled during fine-motor tasks and had difficulty following directions. He was described by his teacher as "active," "likes things his way," and "does not get along well with peers." These difficulties at school added to his parents' developmental concerns leading them to pursue formal medical and educational evaluations.

Christopher was put on Ritalin for a short time (approximately eight weeks) when he was four, but since his parents felt that the medication decreased his interactions with others, increased his perseverations, and "zonked" his overall awareness level, they discontinued the use of the Ritalin.

Formal and Informal Testing

Results of the fine- and gross-motor testing indicated that both areas were delayed. Specific concerns were noted in body awareness and motor planning.

Eligibility for Special Education Services: Preschool

Christopher was determined to be eligible for early childhood special education (ECSE) services and continued to attend the early childhood program in the same classroom for the remainder of the school year. This combined Title I and ECSE classroom was led by an early childhood special education teacher, an early childhood teacher, and a paraeducator. In addition to the special education services, he received physical therapy, occupational therapy, and language therapy as related services. Christopher continued to attend the community preschool program as well, because his parents wanted him to have the opportunity to interact with typical peers. Finally, he received private speech/language and occupational therapy at the children's hospital where he had been evaluated.

Intervention: Preschool

Throughout the evaluative process and his year in the public school preschool program, teachers and related services staff used a number of strategies to address Christopher's educational and sensory needs. Close communication was maintained among teachers, therapists, and parents so they could share and compare notes on both successful and less successful intervention ideas. Educational strategies used with success included visual schedules, priming, social stories, and breaking down tasks into smaller steps that could be accomplished as separate units of a task rather than an entire sequence of units that had to be done until the task was completed. Modeling and scripted role-play helped Chris know what to expect during some of the more challenging preschool events such as field trips, Halloween parties, wearing costumes, trick-or-treating, and sitting on Santa's lap at the mall.

Teachers found that if sensory opportunities were available and incorporated into the planned activities, Christopher was less anxious and more successful in all classroom activities. Sensory activities included opportunities for vestibular and proprioceptive input; walks to get ice, chewing ice and other chewy food or nonfood items, jumping on a trampoline, and playing with resistive materials such as lycra, therapy balls, and Rapper Snappers™.

... if sensory opportunities were available and incorporated into the planned activities, Christopher was less anxious and more successful in all classroom activities.

Christopher was able to request and use fidgets, chewies, weighted objects, and breaks when needed.

Additionally, nonpreferred activities were followed by preferred activities, which resulted in more willingness to participate in less favorite tasks. Preferred activities included looking at books with an adult, working puzzles, and visits to "Miss Kitty" and "Miss Lori" (favorite secretaries at the school).

A variety of interventions were used to support Christopher at home and school. His parents were already incorporating many opportunities for movement at home including hanging a swing in the basement, using a therapy ball, and having him wear ankle weights or putting weights in his backpack. The family invented games such as the "Nestea Plunge" (consisted of falling backwards into the couch cushions from the arm of the couch, just like the commercial) that offered vestibular and proprioceptive input.

Christopher's parents also used their son's strong interest in geography to promote interaction and provide much-needed sensory input. They played a geography game in which Christopher would use his GeoSafari Globe™ and ask to be thrown on a geographic site after answering a question about it. For example, he would say, "Throw me on Madagascar" as he pointed to it on the globe in response to a question about where the island was located. His dad would toss him on the couch cushions, thereby giving him a good dose of vestibular and proprioceptive input. This game would be repeated over and over with Chris being thrown to many obscure geographic locations. The whole family got involved in these games, making it part of a family "sensory" routine. Thus, with input from his teachers and therapists, sensory opportunities were embedded into Christopher's home and school routines.

Additional sensory accommodations at home included: (a) brushing Christopher's teeth while he was in the bathtub, (b) using a teepee and a beanbag chair for resting, (c) offering chewy snacks to discourage chewing on clothing and toys, and (d) using a dry erase board on an easel to provide an upright smooth writing surface for drawing with markers.

Eligibility for Special Education Services: Kindergarten

Approximately one year after he had started the ECSE program, Christopher was referred for evaluation before entering kindergarten in the fall. Additional formal and informal testing was indicated to determine whether continued special education services were needed in kindergarten and to delineate a categorical educational diagnosis. Current guidelines in the state where Chris lives require a categorical label when a child enters kindergarten rather than the more global ECSE label.

Cognitive: An intellectual assessment indicated that Christopher had an IQ score of 83. Strengths were noted in vocabulary, pattern analysis, expressive language, and long-term memory. Weaker areas included comprehension, bead memory, short-term memory (auditory), and understanding absurdities.

Academic/Achievement: Several formal achievement measures were administered to determine Chris' abilities. These showed that he demonstrated strengths in prereading/reading skills and weaker skills in math and writing. All scores fell within his expected age range, however.

Communication: Formal test results indicated strengths in vocabulary skills and use of grammar, and weaknesses in defining words, stating attributes, identifying functions, and pragmatic skills (turn taking, topic maintenance).

Motor Skills: Gross- and fine-motor skills continued to be delayed, with fine-motor skills more delayed than gross-motor skills.

Autism Scales: Due to Christopher's earlier medical diagnosis of PDD-NOS, autism scales were administered to assist with categorical diagnosis. Ratings were requested from parents, his ECSE teacher, and the community preschool teacher. While the results varied somewhat across the measures given, in general, his parents reported less behaviors resembling autism than did the ECSE and community preschool teachers. However, all raters indicated social interaction as the area of most concern.

Note. At the time of this assessment, no tools were available that specifically attempt to identify Asperger Syndrome.

Sensory Processing: The *Sensory Profile* (Dunn, 1999) was administered. Ratings reported reflect his mother's observations of his behaviors. The results indicated that Christopher has sensory processing differences (auditory, touch, oral, and multisensory) and sensory modulation differences related to his difficulties in processing the sensory input he receives, which then impact his emotional and behavioral responses to this input. Some of the behaviors reported as occurring frequently or always included:

- distracted or has trouble functioning if there is a lot of noise
- seeks all kinds of movement, which interferes with daily routines
- expresses distress during grooming
- touches people/objects to the point of irritating others
- has difficulty paying attention
- mouths objects
- has weak grasp
- seems accident prone
- always "on the go"
- displays excessive emotional outbursts when unsuccessful at a task
- handwriting is illegible
- has difficulty tolerating changes in routines
- jumps from one activity to the next so that it interferes with play

These difficulties made it difficult for Christopher to attain and maintain an appropriate level of arousal and regulate his responses to sensory input throughout his daily routines.

Intervention: Kindergarten

When Chris was five, his mother and both occupational therapists working with him attended a "How Does Your Engine Run?" workshop (see Chapter 4). Since Christopher was already interested in trains, the engine concept was right up his alley. Thus, using the words "too fast," "too slow," and "just right" while relating his body to the engine of a train helped Christopher understand his own behavior. Polaroid pictures were taken of him demonstrating "high" (too fast), "just right," and "low" (too slow) to serve as a visual gauge to help Christopher become more aware of his activity levels. Christopher was rarely in "low," however, unless asleep or sick, making it challenging for him to demonstrate this engine level for the picture.

In Christopher's all-day kindergarten program, sensory activities were embedded in the classroom routine. For example, to permit movement breaks and to satisfy his oral needs, trips to the principal to get licorice and ice were used. A visual schedule, which was available to all students in the class, provided routine, and paired preferred tasks (computer or reading) with nonpreferred tasks (writing/cutting/coloring). Since art was a challenging activity for Christopher due to the fine-motor activities involved, a high school volunteer was partnered with him to keep him on task and help him complete art projects. Christopher also spent time in the school's computer lab when he needed a break from the classroom. The "How Does Your Engine Run?" program was implemented in his classroom with some success but it was difficult to implement it consistently.

Christopher initially experienced problems riding the bus from home to school. Specifically, he would chew on the seats of the bus, refused to remain seated, and appeared anxious. At the suggestion of the occupational therapist, Christopher started to wear a heavy backpack on the bus, which contained a 4-5 pound frog beanbag – an intervention that was successful in addressing all three target behaviors.

Occupational and physical therapy, offered both in the classroom and as a pullout service, allowed opportunities for sensory movement and paired skill development with sensory input. For example, Chris enjoyed the swing, ball pit, rolling in the barrel, and jumping on the trampoline. Sessions generally followed a routine that included Chris' participation in a nonpreferred activity followed by a preferred activity. He participated better when tasks incorporated his perseverative interests (trains/computers/books) and included imaginative/role play in which he and the therapist took on a character's name (e.g., "I'm Thomas the Tank Engine; You're Bertie the Red Bus"). The "How Does Your Engine Run?" program was also used successfully in therapy sessions.

Towards the middle of the year, his teacher expressed concern about Christopher's activity level and his ability to follow directions. As a result, his parents consulted with a physician who recommended Ritalin. Although hesitant, Christopher's parents agreed to a trial period of the medication to determine its impact on his school functioning. His teacher reported immediate changes in Christopher's behaviors. Specifically, she noted improvements in attention, turn taking, and the ability to follow multiple-step directions. The medication has been continued, with some breaks during the summer months when Chris was not in school.

Intervention: First Grade

Christopher's parents and staff members who knew him reported that he made great progress during his first-grade year. His teacher embedded frequent sensory and movement breaks within the class routine in which all children participated. Christopher was permitted to use a fidget or to carry a preferred item in class to facilitate calmness. He also frequently carried a stuffed Scooby-Doo dog. In addition, his teacher addressed his oral needs by continuing to provide licorice and ice breaks, as needed. A tent with pillows was set up in the classroom, which served as a "home base" or break area. When Christopher was anxious about changes in the class schedule or a teacher/therapist being absent, he was allowed to sit in the tent and read a book. By the end of the school year, he was better able to handle changes although he was still anxious when the schedule changed or the teacher/therapist was absent. For academics, Christopher's classroom teacher modified written and cutting tasks to include highlighter lines to trace and cut and shortened these tasks, as needed. As Chris began to take an interest in writing, classroom, and therapy-based tasks centered on practicing letter formations.

Visual supports were also used. For example, he referred to a picture schedule to independently pack and unpack his backpack at the beginning and end of the day. Another visual support helped him sequence and complete art activities. A visual schedule was also used to guide him through the required elements to be completed on a computer program so he didn't just "play" with the computer. Finally, a visual "stop" sign was used to help Christopher when he began to perseverate.

Sensory issues continued to be addressed in individual therapy session, although as the year progressed, he less frequently chose sensory activities. He continued to benefit from routine and often stated the way the therapy session should be conducted by saying, "First we ..., and then we ... ."

The staff who worked with Christopher continued to use the terminology from "How Does Your Engine Run?" to help him become more aware of his level of alertness. The program was considered more successful in first grade, as he was now able to describe his own activity levels more accurately.

Peer interactions also improved during first grade. For example, Chris began to talk and play with others at recess and peers came to him for assistance with reading. To keep him improving in this area, therapists involved peers in sessions and included social skills instruction. Also, social stories, which were read by the staff who worked with him, addressed social issues. Concurrently, improvements were seen in turn taking and sustaining an interaction with peers and adults.

Mother's Perspective on Christopher as He Begins Second Grade

As Christopher begins second grade, his mother reflected on the progress he has made. His current interests include Thomas the Tank Engine™, Pokemon™, Digimon™, Scooby-Doo™, and books on tape. He also enjoys Tiger Cubs and swimming. Amusement parks rides, such as roller coasters, continue to be favorites. His strengths include reading, using the computer, telling Scooby-Doo jokes, and putting together puzzles. Skills continue to emerge relative to playing games, taking turns, and interacting with peers. Challenges are still evident in math, talking on the phone, and getting dressed independently.

For purposes of this case study, Christopher's mother completed an updated *Sensory Profile* on her son (see Table 5.1). This showed that Christopher still has some sensory issues. Specifically, he has difficulty changing from long pants to shorts, prefers heavy comforters to sheets, and dislikes wearing shoes. He avoids bright sunlight and won't play outside, especially on a windy day. He continues to be somewhat picky about food textures (specially pork and chicken), but his mother is now able to serve him a plate of food with more than one

Table 5.1

Comparison of Results on the Sensory Profile for Christopher at Prekindergarten and at the Beginning of 2nd Grade

Sensory Profile	Prekindergarten	Entering 2nd Grade
Sensory Processing		
Auditory Processing	Probable difference	Typical performance*
Visual Processing	Typical performance	Typical performance
Vestibular Processing	Typical performance	Typical performance
Touch Processing	Definite difference	Definite difference
Multisensory Processing	Definite difference	Probable difference*
Oral Sensory Processing	Probable difference	Probable difference
Modulation		
Sensory Processing Related to Endurance/Tone	Typical performance	Definite differnce
Modulation Related to Body Position and Movement	Definite difference	Typical performance*
Modulation of Movement Affecting Activity Level	Probable difference	Probable differnce
Modulation of Sensory Input Affecting Emotional Responses	Definite difference	Typical performance*
Modulation of Visual Input Affecting Emotional Responses and Activity Level	Probable difference	Probable difference
Behavior and Emotional Responses		
Emotional/Social Responses	Definite difference	Probable difference*
Behavioral Outcomes of Sensory Processing	Definite difference	Definite difference
Items Indicating Thresholds for Responses	Typical performance	Typical performance

*Items in these areas were rated by Christopher's mother as occurring less frequently now than when he was entering kindergarten.

item on it at a time. As seen in Table 5.1, Chris' sensory issues appear to be less intrusive in his life than they were two years earlier.

The "How Does Your Engine Run?" program is still used at home. Christopher has learned to recognize his state of alertness and to verbalize how he feels. He has incorporated his own vocabulary into the program, telling his parents, "That shirt gives me shivers," or "That makes me nervous." Self-regulation skills have improved with greater awareness, as indicated by his attempts to initiate or request an activity that provides helpful sensory input.

Some of the environmental modifications that Christopher uses at school also are in evidence at home. A visual schedule is posted on his bedroom door and on the bathroom door, and a timer is used to signal the end of computer time. In addition, Christopher's family has established home rules, which are written down and reviewed often. These include:

- Be nice to your family
- Brush your teeth
- Help set the table
- Say "I love you"
- Get dressed
- Check on charts

Christopher has made great progress throughout the years in academics, behavior, and social skills. In each of these areas, sensory issues have been addressed. There is no doubt that given the comprehensive supports that address his sensory needs, Christopher will continue to make great progress!

REFERENCES

Abrash, A. (n.d.). Indicators of sensory processing difficulties. *Clinical Connection, 9*(3), j.

American Psychiatric Association. (1994). *Diagnostic and statistical manual of mental disorders (4th ed.).* Washington, DC: Author.

Asperger, H. (1944). Die 'Autistichen Psychopathen' im Kindersalter. *Archiv für Psychiatrie und Nervenkrankheiten, 117,* 76-136.

Attwood, T. (1998). *Asperger's syndrome: A guide for parents and professionals.* London: Jessica Kingsley.

Ayres, A. J. (1979). *Sensory integration and the child.* Los Angeles: Western Psychological Services.

Ayres, A. J. (1989). *Sensory integration and praxis test.* Los Angeles: Western Psychological Services.

Dunn, W. (1999). *The sensory profile: A contextual measure of children's responses to sensory experiences in daily life.* San Antonio, TX: The Psychological Corporation.

Dunn W. (1999). *Short sensory profile.* San Antonio, TX: The Psychological Corporation.

Dunn, W. (1999, November). *Applied neuroscience: A model for sensory processing in daily life.* Department of Occupational Therapy Colloquium, Kansas City, KS.

Durand, V. M., & Crimmins, D. (1992). *Motivation assessment scale.* Topeka, KS: Monaco.

Hanschu, B. (1998). *Ready approach: Key for interpreting the Sensory Integration Inventory for individuals with developmental disabilities.* Phoenix, AZ: Developmental Concepts.

Henry Occupational Therapy Services, Inc. (1998). *Tool chest: For teachers, parents, and students.* Youngstown, AZ: Author.

Henry Occupational Therapy Services, Inc. (1998). *Tools for students: Tool chest activities for home and school.* Youngstown, AZ: Author.

Henry Occupational Therapy Services, Inc. (1998). *Tools for teachers: Sensory integration in the schools.* Youngstown, AZ: Author.

Kientz, M., & Miller, H. (1999). Classroom evaluation of the child with autism. *AOTA School System Special Interest Section Newsletter, 6*(1), 1-4.

Lyons, J. (1997). *Gather stars for your children: Songs to enhance social skills and to foster a welcoming attitude.* Marietta, GA: Tunes for Knowing and Growing.

Meara, K. (1999). *Central auditory processing in five persons with Asperger Syndrome.* Unpublished master's thesis, University of Kansas.

Miller, L. J., & Lane, S. J. (2000). Toward a consensus in terminology in sensory integration theory and practice: Part 1: Taxonomy of neurophysiological processes. *Sensory Integration Special Interest Section Quarterly, 23*(1), 1-4.

Myles, B. S., Dunn, W., & Orr, S. (2000). *Sensory issues in Asperger Syndrome: A preliminary investigation.* Manuscript submitted for publication.

Myles, B. S., & Simpson, R. L. (1998). *Asperger Syndrome: A guide for educators and parents.* Austin, TX: Pro-Ed.

Myles, B. S., Simpson, R. L., & Bock, S. J. (2000). *Asperger Syndrome diagnostic scale.* Austin, TX: Pro-Ed.

Myles, B. S., & Southwick, J. (1999). *Asperger Syndrome and difficult moments: Practical solutions for tantrums, rage, and meltdowns.* Shawnee Mission, KS: AAPC.

Occupational Therapy Associates. (1997). *Adolescent/adult checklist of occupational therapy.* Watertown, MA: Authors.

Occupational Therapy Associates. (1997). *Early intervention checklist of occupational therapy for infants and toddlers: Ages 0-2.11 years.* Watertown, MA: Authors.

Occupational Therapy Associates. (1997). *Preschool checklist of occupational therapy: Ages 3-4.11 years.* Watertown, MA: Authors.

Occupational Therapy Associates. (1997). *School-age therapy checklist of occupational therapy: Ages 5-12 years.* Watertown, MA: Authors.

Reisman, J., & Hanschu, B. (1992). *Sensory integration – Revised for individuals with developmental disabilities: User's guide.* Hugo, MN: PDP Press.

Williams, M. W., & Shellenberger, S. (1996). *How does your engine run? A leader's guide to the Alert Program for Self-Regulation.* Albuquerque, NM: TherapyWorks.

Wing, L. (1981). Asperger's Syndrome: A clinical account. *Psychological Medicine, 11,* 115-129.

World Health Organization. (1992). *International classification of diseases and related health problems (10th ed.).* Geneva: Author.

Yack, E., Sutton, S., & Aquilla, P. (1998). *Building bridges through sensory integration.* Weston, ONT: Authors.

GLOSSARY

Adaptive response: A response or action that results in successfully meeting an environmental demand (Ayres, 1979).

Auditory perception: The ability to receive, identify, discriminate, understand, and respond to sounds.

Camping pillow: Consists of baffled air chambers that can be blown up to a desirable tension. When you sit on it it allows movement depending on the amount of air. Can be found at outdoor equipment and discount stores. Some people use partially inflated beach balls for the same effect.

Central nervous system (CNS): The part of the nervous system, consisting of the brain and spinal cord, that coordinates the activity of the entire nervous system.

Disc 'O' Sit™: An inflatable disc that enables users to work on posture while seated or to balance in seated or standing positions.

Discrimination: The act of considering details and distinguishing salient features.

Dycem: A synthetic flat covering material that provides a nonslip surface.

"Fright, flight, or fight" response: A nervous system defensive response to real or perceived danger.

Gustatory: The sensory system that distinguishes taste.

Mapping: Making sense of details provided through the sensory systems.

Modulation: The brain's regulation of its own activity.

Olfactory: The sensory system that allows for discrimination and association of odors.

Proprioception: The unconscious perception of sensations coming from one's joints, muscles, tendons, and ligaments that allow the brain to know where each body part is and how it is moving.

Tactile: The sense of touch. Receptors in the skin that allow this sensory system to perceive sensations of pressure, vibration, movement, temperature and pain.

Theraputty™: Resistant manipulative putty that can be kneaded and pulled with one or both hands.

Threshold: The point at which neurological impulses trigger an action or response.

T-stool: Seating surface with only one leg for support. Variations can be found in therapy catalogs, outdoor equipment stores, as well as homemade options.

Theraband™/theratubing: One of many tubings available in various degrees of resistance and tension. Latex-free options should be considered.

Vestibular: The sensory system that responds to the position of the head and body movement and coordinates movements of the eyes, head, and body. Receptors are located in the inner ear.

Visual: The system that allows us to interpret information about our environment through various types of perception (depth, spatial orientation, etc.); also serves to reinforce other types of sensory input.

RESOURCES

Books

Anderson, E., & Emmons, P. (1996). *Unlocking the mysteries of sensory dysfunction.* Arlington, TX: Future Horizons.

Anderson, J. (1998). *Sensory motor issues in autism.* San Antonio, TX: Therapy Skill Builders.

Anzelmo, M. E., & Bonanni, D. M. (1997). *Building block to communication: Oral motor and speech skills for infants, toddlers, and preschoolers.* San Antonio, TX: Communication Skill Builders.

Baker, B., & Brightman, A. (1997). *Steps to independence: Teaching everyday skills to children with special needs.* Baltimore: Brookes Publishing.

Beninghof, A. (1998). *SenseAble strategies: Including diverse learners through multisensory strategies.* Longmont, CO: Sopris West.

Bittinger, G. (1997). *Multisensory theme-a-saurus: Learning through the five senses.* Everett, WA: Totline Publications.

Blanche, E. I., Botticelli, T. M., & Hallway, M. K. (1995). *Combining neuro-developmental treatment and sensory integration principles: An approach to pediatric therapy.* San Antonio, TX: Therapy Skill Builders.

Byte, K. (1996). *Classroom intervention for the school-based therapist: An integrated model.* San Antonio, TX: Therapy Skill Builders.

Chandler, B. E. (1997). *The essence of play: A child's occupation.* Bethesda, MD: The American Occupational Therapy Association.

Cleveland, A., Canton, B., & Adler, L. (1994). *Activities unlimited.* Elgin, IL: Building Blocks.

Crawford, J., Hanson, J., Gums, M., & Neys, P. (1994). *Please teach all of me: Multisensory activities for preschoolers.* Longmont, CO: Sopris West.

DeGangi, G. (1994). *Documenting sensorimotor progress: A pediatric therapist's guide.* San Antonio, TX: Therapy Skill Builders.

Dennison, P., & Dennison, G. (1986). *Brain gym.* Ventura, CA: Edu-Kinesthetics.

Dennison, P., & Dennison, G. (1986). *Brain gym: Teachers edition, revised.* Ventura, CA: Edu-Kinesthetics.

Duke, M. P., Nowicki, S., & Martin, E. A. (1996). *Teaching your child the language of social success.* Atlanta, GA: Peachtree.

Duran, G., & Klenke-Ormiston, S. (1994). *Multi-okay: Sensory activities for school readiness.* San Antonio, TX: Therapy Skills Builders.

Freed, J., & Parsons, L. (1997). *Right-brained children in a left-brained world: Unlocking the potential of your ADD child.* New York: Simon & Schuster.

Frick, S., Frick, R., Oetter, P., & Richter, E. (1996). *Out of the mouths of babes: Discovering the developmental significance of the mouth.* Hugo, MN: PDP Press.

Ganz, J. (1998). *Including SI: A guide to using sensory integration concepts in the school environment.* Bohemia, NY: Kapable Kids.

Haldy, M., & Haack, L. (1995). *Making it easy: Sensorimotor activities at home and school.* San Antonio, TX: Therapy Skills Builders.

Hammeken, P. (1995). *Inclusion: 450 strategies for success.* Minnetonka, MN: Peytral.

Hannaford, C. (1995). *Smart moves: Why learning is not all in your head.* Arlington, CA: Great Ocean Publishers.

Henry, D. (1998). *Tool chest for teachers, parents, and students: A handbook to facilitate self-regulation.* Youngtown, AZ: Henry Occupational Therapy Services.

Herring, K. L., & Wilkinson, S. (1995). *Action alphabet: Sensorimotor activities for groups.* San Antonio, TX: Therapy Skill Builders.

Holland, T., & Roberts, L. (1992). *Push-in: An integrated program for teachers and occupational therapists.* New Hartford, NY: Oneida Board of Cooperative Education Services.

Holzschuher, C. (1997). *How to manage your inclusive classroom.* Huntington Beach, CA: Teacher Created Materials.

Inamura, K. (1998). *SI for early intervention: A team approach.* San Antonio, TX: Therapy Skill Builders.

Kane, K., & Anderson, M. (1998). *PT activities for pediatric groups.* San Antonio, TX: Therapy Skill Builders.

Kasser, S. L. (1995). *Inclusive games: Movement for everyone.* Champaign, IL: Human Kinetics.

Koomar, J., & Friedman, B. (1992). *The hidden senses: Your muscle sense.* Rockville, MD: The American Occupational Therapy Association.

Koomar, J., & Friedman, B. (1992). *The hidden senses: Your balance sense.* Rockville, MD: The American Occupational Therapy Association.

Kranowitz, C. (1998). *The out of sync child: Recognizing and coping with sensory integration dysfunction.* New York: Skylight Press.

Landin, L. (1994). *100 blackboard games revised.* Carthage, IL: Fearon Teacher Aids.

Mackie, E. (1996). *Oral-motor activities for young children.* East Moline, IL: LinguiSystems.

Metzner, S. (1968). *One-minute game guide.* Carthage, IL: Fearon Teacher Aids.

Morris, L. R., & Schulz, L. (1989). *Creative play activities for children with disabilities.* Champaign, IL: Human Kinetic Books.

Neville, H., & Johnson, D. (1998). *Temperament tools: Working with your child's inborn traits.* Seattle, WA: Parenting Press.

Oetter, P., Richter, E. W., & Frick, S. M. (1988). *MORE: Integrating the mouth with sensory and postural functions.* Hugo, MN: PDP Press.

Orr, C. (1998). *Mouth madness: Oral motor activities for children.* San Antonio, TX: Therapy Skill Builders.

Scheerer, C. (1997). *Sensorimotor groups: Activities for school and home.* San Antonio, TX: Therapy Skill Builders.

Schwartz, S., & Heller, J. E. (1996). *The new language of toys: Teaching communication skills to children with special needs.* Bethesda, MD: Woodbine House.

Sheda, C. H., & Ralston, P. R. (1997). *Sensorimotor processing activity plans.* San Antonio, TX: Therapy Skills Builders.

Sher, B. (1996). *Different drummers – Same song: 400 inclusion games that promote cognitive skills.* San Antonio, TX: Therapy Skill Builders.

Sher, B. (1997). *Moving right along.* Hugo, MN: PDP Press.

Sheridan, S. (1998). *Why don't they like me? Helping your child make and keep friends.* Longmont, CO: Sopris West.

Thompson, S. (1997). *The source for nonverbal learning disabilities.* East Moline, IL: LinguiSystems, Inc.

Tobias, C. (1994). *The way they learn: How to discover and teach to your child's strengths.* Colorado Springs, CO: Focus on the Family Publishing.

Trinnaman, R. (1994). *The way they learn: How to discover and teach to your child's strengths.* Colorado Springs, CO: Focus on the Family Publishing.

Tupper, L. C., & Klosterman-Miesner, K. E. (1995). *School hardening: Sensory integration strategies for class and home.* San Antonio, TX: Therapy Skill Builders.

Wilbarger, P., & Wilbarger, J. (1991). *Sensory defensiveness in children aged 2-12: An intervention guide for parents and other caretakers.* Denver, CO: Avanti Educational Programs.

Williams, M. W., & Shellenberger, S. (1996). *How does your engine run? A leader's guide to the Alert Program for Self-Regulation.* Albuquerque, NM: TherapyWorks.

Wilmes, L., & Wilmes, D. (1996). *2's experience sensory play.* Elgin, IL: Building Blocks.

Winebrenner S. (1996). *Teaching kids with learning difficulties in the regular classroom.* Minneapolis, MN: Free Spirit.

RESOURCES
Toys and Materials

Abledata
8455 Colesville Rd., Suite 935
Silver Spring, MD 20910-3319
800-227-0216
abledata.com

Listings of over 19,000 products for individuals with disabilities, including information about toys for children with special needs.

Achievement Products, Inc.
P.O. Box 9033
Canton, OH 44711
800-373- 4699
AchievementProductsInc.com

Catalog of special education and rehabilitation equipment for children with special needs from birth to 18.

Antoni Toys and Products
232 S.E. Oak St., Suite 103
Portland, OR 97214
800-826-8664
nas.com/downsyn.toy

Appropriate toys and play materials for any child, but especially for children with physical disabilities.

Autism Resource Network, Inc.
5123 Westmill Rd.
Minnetonka, MN 55345
612-988-0088
autismbooks.com

Books and materials with emphasis on AS and autism.

Brookes Publishing Co.
P.O. Box 10624
Baltimore, MD 21285-0624
800-638-3775
brookespublishing.com

Resources for books on various disabilities as well as assessment and intervention methodology.

Childgarden
P.O. Box 15023
St. Louis, MO 63110
800-726-4769
childgarden.com

Pillows, cuddle-ups (large-sized pillows that look like animals/bugs).

Childswork/Childsplay Center
P.O. Box 61586
King of Prussia, PA 19406
800-962-1141
childswork.com

A catalog designed to address the mental health needs of children and families through play with books, board games, puppets, posters, videos, dolls, and doll houses.

Chime Time
One Sportime Way
Atlanta, GA 30340
800-477-5075
orders@sportime.com

Catalog of bright, soft, sturdy, colorful building blocks and textured balls.

Communication Skill Builders, Inc.
555 Academic Ct.
San Antonio, TX 78204-2498
800-211-8378
hbtpc.com

Therapy resources and books with an emphasis on communication.

Community Playthings
P.O. Box 901
Rifton, NY 12471-0901
800-777-4244
communityproducts.com

Although not specially designed for children with special needs, many of the products may be of interest.

Constructive Playthings
1227 East 119th St.
Grandview, MO 64030-1117
816-761-5900
constplay.com

Although not specially designed for children with special needs, many of the products may be of interest.

Creative Educational Surplus
1000 Apollo Rd.
Eagan, MN 55121-2240
800-886-6428
creativesurplus.com

Art materials, containers, Velcro, and other useful items.

Crestwood Company
6625 N. Sidney Place
Milwaukee, WI 53209-3259
414-352-5678
communicationaids.com

Communication aids for children

and adults. The catalog contains a section of adapted toys (switches must be purchased separately).

Don Johnston, Inc.
P.O. Box 639
1000 N. Rand Rd., Bldg. 115
Wauconda, IL 60084
800-999-4660
donjohnston.com

Computer software, hardware, and switches.

Dragon Fly Toy Company
291 Yale Ave.
Winnipeg, MB R3M 0L4
Canada
800-308-2208
dragonflytoys.com

Toys and related products for people with special play needs.

Enabling Devices
Toys for Special Children
385 S. Warbuton Ave
Hastings-on-Hudson, NY 10706
800-832-8697
enablingdevices.com

Adapted toys for children with special needs.

Lakeshore Learning Materials
2965 E. Dominques
Carson, CA 90749
800-421-5354
lakeshorelearning.com

Educational products, adaptive equipment, and outdoor play equipment.

Mayer-Johnson Co.
P.O. Box 1579
Solana Beach, CA 92075-7579
800-588-4548
mayer-johnson.com

Communication system software (great for PECS systems), including books, materials and resources.

One Step Ahead
P.O. Box 517
Lake Bluff, IL 60044
800-274-8440
onestepahead.com

Although not specifically designed for children with special needs, many of the products may be of interest (for children from newborn through kindergarten age).

Oriental Trading Company, Inc.
P.O. Box 2308
Omaha, NE 68103-2308
800-228-2269
oriental.com

Inexpensive bulk items great for reinforcers, fidgets, and other sensory needs.

Oppenheim Toy Portfolio
40 E. 9th St., Suite 14M
New York, NY 10003
800-544-8697
titlegoco.com

A full chapter in their book, The Best Toys, Books, Videos, and Software for Kids, *is dedicated to choosing and using ordinary toys for kids with special needs. Publishes a quarterly newsletter that includes a section on adapting toys.*

OTideas, Inc.
124 Morris Turnpike
Randolph, NJ 07869
973-895-3622
otideas.com

Therapy materials and resources.

PDP Products
P.O. Box 2009
Stillwater, MN 55082
651-439-8865
pdppro.com

Books, sensory materials for fidgets, and fun toys.

Pediatric Projects
P.O. Box 571555
Tarzana, CA
800-947-0947
pediatricmentalhealth.org

Nonprofit organization that has information on over 500 toys and books that have been developed to explain medical conditions to children.

Perfectly Safe
The Catalog Designed for
Parents Who Care
7245 Whipple Ave. NW
North Canton, OH 44270
800-837-KIDS (5437)
kidsstuff.com

Although not specifically designed for children with special needs, many of the products may be of interest; all are designed to ensure child safety.

Play with a Purpose
220 24th Ave. NW
P.O. Box 998
Owatonna, MN 55060-0998
800-533-0446
gophersport.com

*Toys, materials, and games that
emphasize physical development
gross-motor and fine-motor skills
and play.*

Prentke-Romich Company
1022 Heyl Rd.
Wooster, OH 44691
800-262-1990
prentrom.com

*Communication and therapy for
individuals with special needs.*

Pro-Ed
8700 Shoal Creek Blvd.
Austin, TX 78757-6897
800-897-3202
proedinc.com

*Tests, reference books, journals, etc.,
used in educational settings.*

**Raymond Geddes and
Company, Inc.**
P.O. Box 24829
Baltimore, MD 21220-0829
800-533-6273
raymondgeddes.com

*Inexpensive items, stickers, pencil
toppers, and fidgets for sensory
needs.*

Rifton Equipment
P.O. Box 901, Route 213
Rifton, NY 12471
800-777-4244
communityproducts.com

*Specialized equipment for children
with disabilities.*

Sammons Preston
An AbilityOne Company
P.O. Box 5071
Bolingbrook, IL 60440-5071
800-323-5547
sammonspreston.com

*Positioning, seating, mobility, and
recreational and adaptive devices for
individuals with special needs.*

S & S Opportunities
P.O. Box 513
Colchester, CT 06415-0513
800-266-8856
snswwide.com

*Equipment and supplies for parents,
educators, and therapists.*

SmileMakers
P.O. Box 2543
Spartanburg, SC 29304
800-825-8085
smilemakers.com

*Fidgets, stickers, small sensory
items, and reinforcers at inexpensive
prices.*

Southpaw Enterprises, Inc.
P.O. Box 1047
Dayton, OH 45401-1047
800-228-1698
southpawenterprises.com

Catalog of sensory integration and developmental therapy products.

Sportime/Abilitiations
One Sportime Way
Atlanta, GA 30340
800-850-8602
abilitations.com

Recreation and exercise products.

Switchworks
P.O. Box 64764
Baton Rouge, LA 70896
225-925-8926

Adapted toys.

TherAdapt
17W 163 Oak Lane
Bensenville, IL 60106
800-261-4919

Adaptive seating and positioning equipment.

Therapeutic Toys Inc.
P.O. Box 418
Moodus, CT 06469-0418
800-638-0676

Adapted toys as well as playground equipment.

Therapro
225 Arlington St.
Framingham, MA 01702-8723
800-257-5376
theraproducts.com

Catalog of resources/materials for parents, educators, and therapists.

Therapy Skill Builders
555 Academic Ct.
San Antonio, TX 78204-2498
800-211-8378
hbtpc.com

Books and material resources that focus on occupational, physical, and speech therapy assessment and interventions.

Toy Manufacturers of America
200 Fifth Ave., Suite 740
New York, NY 10010
212-675-1141
toy-tma.org

Toy resource catalog entitled, Guide to Toys for Children Who Are Blind or Visually Impaired.

World Games
P.O. Box 517
Colchester, CT 06415-0517
800-243-9232
snswide.com

Specially designed and adapted board games and activities for recreation and therapy.

RESOURCES

Organizations

**American Occupational
Therapy Association, Inc.**
4720 Montgomery Lane
Bethesda, MD 20824-1220
301-652-AOTA or
1-800-668-8255
aota.org

**American Physical Therapy
Association**
1111 North Fairfax St.
Alexandria, VA 22314-1488
703-684-2782
apta.org

**American Speech-Language-
Hearing Association**
10801 Rockville Pike
Rockville, MD 20852
301-897-5700 or 800-638-TALK
asha.org

**Asperger Syndrome Coalition
of the United States**
P.O. Box 9267
Jacksonville Beach, FL
32240-9267
904-745-6741
asperger.org

**Autism Society of America
(ASA)**
7910 Woodmont Ave., Suite 300
Bethesda, MD 20814-3015
800-3AUTISM
autism-society.org

**Center for Neuro-
developmental Studies, Inc.**
5430 West Glenn Dr.
Glendale, AZ 85301-2628
623-915-0345
cirs.org/homepage/cns

**Council for Exceptional
Children (CEC)**
1920 Association Dr.
Reston, VA 22091
703-620-3660
cecsped.org

Geneva Center for Autism
250 Davisville Ave., Suite 200
Toronto, Ontario
Canada M4S 1H2
416-322-7877
autism.net

**Online Asperger Syndrome
Information and Support
(O.A.S.I.S.)**
Maintained by Barb Kirby
Made possible by the
University of Delaware
udel.edu/bkirby/asperger

**Sensory Integration
International (SII)**
1602 Cabrillo Ave.
Torrance, CA 90501
310-320-9986
sensoryint.com

Sensory Integration Resource Center (SInetwork)
The KID Foundation
1901 West Littleton Boulevard
Littleton, CO 80120
sinetwork.org

Therapy Skill Builders
The Psychological Corporation
555 Academic Ct.
San Antonio, TX 78204-2498
800-211-8378
psychcorp.com

TherapyWorks Inc.
4901 Butte Pl., NW
Albuquerque, NM 87120
505-897-3478
alertprogram.com

Western Psychological Services
Sensory Integration Training
12031 Wilshire Blvd.
Los Angeles, CA 90025-1251
800-648-8857
wpspublish.com

Many of the national organizations have state chapters. Each national organization can give you information about your state's chapter.

INDEX